F. H. Engelsdorfer

The Soul of Frederick W. Robertson

Sincerely & gratefully yours
Fred W Robertson

To

THE THREE ANDREWS

Father, Son, and

Grandson

Contents

Introduction

ROBERTSON of Brighton has long held the title of "the preacher's preacher." After his death in 1853 he began to be widely known because of his published sermons. In 1865 he won still more acclaim through the publication of two volumes by Stopford A. Brooke, *Life and Letters of Fred. W. Robertson.* That standard biography has long since gone out of print. Four books of Robertson's sermons have recently become available in a single volume at a modest price.[1] Hence the time seems to have come for a new book about Robertson of Brighton. The present volume deals with his life and sermons, rather than his letters.

This new work should appeal to every lover of preaching. Many of us who teach homiletics think of Robertson as the most influential preacher thus far in the English-speaking world. We may not always agree with him, doctrinally. We may feel more affection for Phillips Brooks, personally. But we look on the young clergyman of Brighton as our chief homiletical influence. In fact, one could prepare a book about the influence of Robertson on later pulpit masters, including many in our own day. For example, think of those who follow his counsel, "Preach suggestively, not exhaus-

---

[1] See *Sermons,* Preached at Brighton, by the late Frederick W. Robertson (New York: Harper & Brothers).

tively." Think too of those who often speak in the pulpit about disorders of the soul.

Among Robertson's many admirers we may single out two. The first will be A. B. Davidson, of Edinburgh, master interpreter of the Old Testament. When a friend "asked whose sermons he cared most to read, he mentioned Robertson's of Brighton. For between Davidson in middle life and Robertson, whose spirit burned out soon, there were strongly marked affinities—the same ardent temperament, the same thirst for reality, the same inexorable conscience, the same individuality, combined with freedom from egotism, the same absorbing sense of God."[2]

Listen also to Dr. Harry Emerson Fosdick: "One of the greatest preachers in the English-speaking world was Robertson of Brighton in the Nineteenth Century. We modern preachers still prime our pumps with his Sermons, because they contain so much permanent suggestiveness. Like every other great believer, he had to fight for his faith and draw himself together around the few things that he found certain. Because he did that, his certainty grew and heightened until he became one of the shining peaks of English-speaking Christianity."

This man deserves to be still better known. Especially does he bring a message for our days of world reconstruction. From Robertson one can learn how to look upon life as it appears in the eyes of God. In the new guidebook and in the Sermons any pastor can enjoy at home a "refresher course." If a minister were merely a dealer in second-hand wares he might turn to the Sermons for something to help fill up the allotted time next Sunday morning. But the local representa-

---

[2] See *Andrew Bruce Davidson* (a biography), by James Strahan (London: 1917), p. 194.

tive of God wants something far better. From Robertson he can gain inspiration to use the Scriptures in meeting the needs of the lay friend in the pew.

This new book will also help those of us who teach homiletics. Some of us have tried all sorts of methods. We now give the preference to the study of sermons by the masters. We have begun to question the value of our cheap and easy excursions into the history of preaching. Why should we ask our students to board a streamlined train and rush through the past at ninety miles an hour? Can we wonder that some of them go into their lifework without having read the sermons of a single master? At least they ought to know the Sermons Preached at Brighton. Why not single out this portion of the homiletical world and tarry here until the students feel at home?

The plan works in various ways. No one would dream of approaching the Sermons of Robertson in the same fashion as those of Spurgeon, or of Bushnell. As a rule the quest begins with the man's biography. Then the student goes through the master's lectures about preaching, if he has left such a volume. Robertson never prepared such a work, partly because he died before he began to be famous. But with such a guidebook as the one now in hand any student can learn all he needs to know before he starts to work on Robertson's Sermons. There he becomes acquainted with the field as a whole. Then he singles out representative discourses of different kinds. These he studies intensively, each according to a tone color all its own. Such a way of working may seem slow, but it brings to light the basic truths about our art.

In this kind of "laboratory work" one encounters a difficulty at the start. How can one single out those "representative discourses"? Among the ninety-three Sermons

Preached at Brighton one discovers all sorts of alluring leads. But a man has to begin somewhere. Why not start with "Christian Progress by Oblivion of the Past"? In various forms this message has sounded out from many a pulpit. The stress falls on the wisdom of "forgetting those things which are behind," and on the duty of "reaching forth unto those things which are before." Next one may turn to "The Principle of the Spiritual Harvest." "Whatsoever a man soweth, that shall he also reap." "Not something else," as Robertson insists, "but *that!*"

Then the trail may lead to "Elijah," a case study of Despondency. From "The Doubt of Thomas" one may go on to "Joseph's Forgiveness of His Brethren." One may deal with "The Illusiveness of Life," or with "The Irreparable Past." The studies in Robertson may close with perhaps the ablest of all the ninety-three sermons, the one about "The Loneliness of Christ." Where in eight discourses could one find more in the way of variety and of uplift? Not only did the preacher use his brains and his imagination. The man who follows him, even from afar, must be willing to leave the beaten track and to wend his way up into the mountains. There he will come face to face with God, and learn God's will for life on earth today.

Up until now the study of Robertson's Sermons has suffered from the lack of a suitable guidebook. This need our young author has met. During his second year at the divinity school he began to enjoy the Sermons Preached at Brighton. Afterwards this love for the works of Robertson led to a Master's thesis. That thesis has provided the substance of the present volume. In preparing the thesis the young writer did scholarly work. He did not merely make a compilation of other men's opinions. He delved into the sources, so that his bibliography extended over twelve pages, and that without padding. As a lover of history and literature, he used brains and imagination, rather than scissors and paste.

The present book differs from the thesis. Here the author wishes to be popular. He hopes that the work will appeal to laymen as well as ministers. From his father's point of view the son has planned wisely, and he has written well. Both with the thesis and with the book the father has had little to do, directly. The son alone bears the responsibility for everything that follows this Introduction. He in turn has leaned heavily upon the written work of Robertson, and less heavily upon that of Stopford A. Brooke. Thus the young writer has given us a popular introduction to a personality well worth knowing, and to a preacher well worth hearing.

In short, this new book should appeal to all who feel young at heart. A hundred years ago, when Robertson went to Brighton in 1847, he was thirty-one years of age. There he did all of his work in six years. Stopford A. Brooke completed the *Life and Letters* when thirty-three years of age. The author of the present book finished the work before he had reached the age of twenty-nine. Thus the young minister of today interprets the young master of yesterday. The two must differ in many other respects, but they seem to be alike in love for the Book of Books, and in loyalty to the Young Man of Galilee, who chose to become the Young Man of Golgotha.

ANDREW WATTERSON BLACKWOOD, SR.

The Soul of Frederick W. Robertson

I

The Call of the Church

The deep interest of biography consists in this—that it is in some measure the description to us of our own inner history. You cannot unveil the secrets of another heart without at the same time finding something to correspond with, and perchance explain, the mysteries of your own. Heart answers here to heart. Between the wisest and the worst there are ten thousand points of marvellous resemblance; and so the trials, the frailties, the bitterness of any human soul, faithfully traced out, ever shadow to us a portraiture of our own experience.

FREDERICK W. ROBERTSON

A DOG was barking. In a home nearby a girl lay sick, and she could not sleep because of the disturbance. Her mother therefore sent a note suggesting that the owners silence their dog. The reply was so gracious in manner that she visited her unknown neighbors to express her thanks. Thus Lady Trench first met Captain Robertson, who had answered the note, and the members of the Robertson family. She especially noticed the eldest son, Frederick, twenty-one years of age. His dog had done the barking.

Frederick W. Robertson marked this trifling occurrence

in Cheltenham, England, in the late thirties of the nineteenth century, as the first event in his call to the ministry. Acquaintance led to friendship with Lady Trench, and friendship led to visits in her home. There Frederick met the Anglican clergyman, Mr. Davies. In the normal way of conversation, the clergyman asked the young man what he intended to do with his life. Robertson answered that he had long since applied for service in the army. The more Mr. Davies talked with him, however, the more the minister saw the traits of a soldier of Christ. As the two came to know each other well, the older man observed Frederick's mild though firm evangelical views, his constant reading of the Bible, and his cheerfulness. He asked Robertson if he had thought of dedicating these gifts to the Christian ministry. Others had also made the suggestion, but Frederick had set his aim: he wanted an army post, not the ordination of the Church of England.

Captain Robertson had served with the Royal Artillery, but he wanted nothing more than to see his son enter the ministry. He and his wife were religious folk of the evangelical type. Their home was Christian. They saw, as only parents can see, their son's purity, intellectual refinement, and deep religious convictions; and they did not care to have these talents, nurtured through the years, wasted in a barracks. He was an obedient, truthful son; an affectionate older brother to three boys and three girls in the family; and a staunch friend of his schoolmates. His parents had watched Frederick grow, like the boy Jesus, in wisdom and stature, gradually and gently awaking to an awareness of life and its beauty. Now that he was a young man, his father and mother prayed that he should give his life to the Church. But when Captain Robertson asked Frederick if he wished to become a minister, his son replied: "Anything but that: I am not fit for it."

Three years before, when he was eighteen, Frederick had announced his choice of a lifework; but he had made the decision even earlier. His heart was in the army. He wanted to be like his father and grandfather before him, a soldier. All his life he had lived near military sound and bustle. "I was rocked and cradled to the roar of artillery," he said, "and the very name of such things sounds to me like home." His earliest memories traced back to Leith Fort, near Edinburgh, in the land of his Scottish forefathers.

"My pony, and my cricket, and my rabbits, and my father's pointers, and the days when I proudly carried his game-bag, and my ride home with the old gamekeeper by moonlight in the frosty evenings, and the boom of cannon, and my father's orderly, the artilleryman who used to walk with me hand-in-hand—these are my earliest recollections."

He loved the rattle of officers' swords and the clink of spurs, but more than these, the table talk of soldiers, barracks incidents, campaigns fought again on winter evenings before the fire, and rumors that traveled fast when soldiers met. His ears were tuned to martial strains.

Frederick venerated his Grandfather Robertson, a soldier who had resisted the French attack on Jersey. When the governor had all but surrendered the island, when the leader died in the defense, and when the second in command also fell, Robertson took charge, and through heavy fighting scored a victory. Frederick's father also went through the baptism of fire. He sailed on Nelson's "Victory" in pursuit of the Toulon squadron. He fought in the War of 1812, and at Hampton, Virginia, stormed and captured the last defensive fieldpiece. The grandfather, the father, and afterward the three younger brothers, all were officers in His Majesty's army. If Frederick thought of himself as a soldier, he could not help himself. Soldiering was in his blood.

He had apparently no desire to become a minister; his father did not want him to put on uniform. What then? Another possible opening for a young Englishman of talent was a legal career. He therefore began the study of law at Bury St. Edmunds, in flat Suffolk, working in the office of a country solicitor. He found the routine slow and dull. Technicalities, precedents, and laws of evidence he loathed, and he shrank from "pettyfogging and professional lying." He had been a normally healthy boy, who liked to tramp over the hills with his father, or play active games with his friends. But in an office, perched in one spot day after day, his body began to fail. One year of law was enough. He left the office, and went back to his parents' home in Cheltenham. He was in poor health.

Soon, however, his body and spirits rallied. Captain Robertson then applied in his son's name for a commission with the Horse Guards. At first the application was refused; Frederick was too young. When finally his name was entered on a list for a cavalry regiment, he was "prodigal of happiness." He threw all his strength, now keyed up by the promise of action, into self-training for the army. Riding horseback by the hour, practicing marksmanship, and slaving over a draughtsman's board, he did all that he could to make himself a useful officer. He was to serve in India; he pored over maps of the country, read its history, and studied its people and problems. He took part imaginatively in the British campaigns of the Sikh war, and reviewed the battles of Sir Charles Napier, a personal friend of his father. The days were full of happy anticipation.

There was a flush of romantic excitement in all this drill. Young Robertson wanted to live daringly, and if need be, to die gloriously. He pictured the men of the dragoons, sabers drawn, charging a stronghold, and he wished himself among them. What could be more valiant than to fall in the rush of battle?—to hear the hail of shot hissing by, feel a bullet pierce his flesh, hang in mid-air for a long, sickening second; then a crash—a sheet of flame—darkness—and "the lineaments of humanity crushed beneath the tramp of the war horse." It was not mere gore that lured him: it was the chivalry of knighthood, defending the Crown, redressing human wrong, and denying self and selfish aims in obedience to a higher loyalty. He thought of the soldier's duty as voluntary sacrifice of the one for the sake of the many.

At the same time he had less romantic longings. He was imaginative, but also thoughtful. His ideal of military life was not simply to spill blood, whether the enemy's or his own. He determined to become "the Cornelius of the regiment." He saw no reason why a soldier could not at the same time be a Christian. Was his father not a religious person? And his grandfather? Everyone warned him against the excesses of barracks life; but he foresaw the temptations clearly, or thought that he could see them. During these months of preparation he wrote a poem, suggested by Wordsworth's "The Happy Warrior," in which he gave his conception of the Christian as no idler, nor dreamer:

> . . . Other far is he,
> The Happy Warrior I would wish to be,
> Amid the scoffs profane, the ribald jeers,
> And worse, the scornful silence of his peers,
> He dares to stand confest, not all untried,
> A lowly servant of the Crucified.

The months lengthened into a year, then two years. He suspected that his application had been lost in some war office pigeonhole; and he wondered if he would ever join the Guards. His parents had given him food, clothes, and a place to live, but he could not be a parasite on their generosity all his life. He began to raise an old question that he once thought settled. What of the Church—after all? It may have been premonition that turned him at the end of the first year to religious books. He added theological works to his military science, and read alternately on ancient wars and Biblical prophecy. In his commonplace book he dwelt at length on the warfare of the spirit. Perhaps he did not sense the fact, but the tide had begun to turn.

At the close of the second long year of waiting, in March, 1837, Lady Trench introduced Frederick Robertson to Mr. Davies. From that meeting, which looked like chance, there followed a complete change in a human destiny. "If I had not met a certain person, I should not have changed my profession: if I had not known a certain lady, I should not probably have met this person: if that lady had not had a delicate daughter who was disturbed by the barking of my dog: if my dog had not barked that night, I should now have been in the dragoons, or fertilising the soil of India."

The decision to enter religious service, however, lay with the father. Captain Robertson advised his son to reconsider the Church. The day after his father spoke to him his mind was wide ajar to the new possibility; then he chanced to speak with another minister, who asked him if he still were set on entering the army. Frederick honestly did not know. After some conversation he asked, "What do you advise me to do?" The answer came back, "Do as your father likes, and pray to God to direct your father aright." Once more Frederick talked over the problem with his father, and in the end left the choice to him.

Young Robertson practiced the military ideal in his home. He knew that military life is above all one of obedience. As a grown son living in his father's house he had not taken orders for years; yet when the time came, he was ready to obey. He had grown from childhood thinking that no one was better or wiser than his father. He was prepared for "immediate, prompt obedience; no questioning 'Why?'" There was no need to place the advantages of the Church over against the disadvantages of the army. There was no reason to trim and balance his motives. Frederick Robertson was never flabby or pliant: if anything he was virile, independent, and self-assertive. He followed his father's decision exactly as a soldier heeds the command of a superior. His father decided on the Church.

But he made his father's choice his own. He never forgot his desire to become a soldier; the years none the less directed his thoughts toward other duties. He wrote from the active labors of the pastorate: "As I walked home in my dragoon cloak, I thought that I ought to be at this moment lying in it at rest at Moodkee, where the Third fought so gallantly, and where spots of brighter green than usual are the only record to mark where the flesh of heroes is melting into its kindred dust again; but in this, as in all other things, a man must reap what he has sown. I believe the spirit of exceeding self-devotion, as a mere romantic instinct, is but folly. Your reward is the satisfaction of finding that you have lost all and gained nothing as well as done nothing. Your thanks are reproach and blame, and you begin to find, when it is too late, that wisdom and prudence alone can redeem even self-sacrifice from the worthless class of mere blind instinct."

Robertson came to feel that the Christian is the only con-
queror deserving of the name. He found places of conflict
other than the battlefield, weapons other than artillery and
firearms, and victory that did not end in dust and smoke. He
learned that the ministry was a sad and frequently disheart-
ening task: yet for that reason not less but more heroic than
riding saddle in the dragoons: "A young man forms ideals
of excellence for himself—only by degrees does he appreciate
Christ. Dazzled by military life, he wishes to fall in a cavalry
charge; he knows nothing higher, till the time comes when he
begins to feel that to save men's lives is better than to destroy
life. *This is the true heroic.* . . . From all types of human
excellence I have made my choice for life and death—Christ."

In 1837, the first year of Victoria's reign, he passed his
examinations for entrance to Oxford. Five days later he
received a letter offering him a commission in the Second
Dragoons, with an option of exchange to the Third, then
about to sail for India. Robertson still could have entered
military service; he went to Oxford instead; and he made
the decision with his eyes fully open. At least no one could
say that he sought refuge in the Church because he could not
get into the army. But he knew then, and he never ceased to
feel, that he had given up the one thing he most desired.

II

The Years of Preparation

BRASENOSE COLLEGE, Oxford, was a somber place. Its outer stonework resembled a fortress, and its smoke-stained rooms were correspondingly stern and gloomy. When Robertson passed through the tower gateway there was little in the surroundings to cheer him. He had the mysterious medley of feeling that attends each new adventure in life: a sense of relief on his final decision to enter the ministry; a shy respect for the upper classmen; a burst of enthusiasm for his new studies; a dread that his training at a Yorkshire grammar school, a French seminary, and an Edinburgh academy would fail to meet the demands of Oxford. Robertson was anxious to begin his classical studies. At first he attended lectures sixteen hours a week. He labored over his notebooks, and began to fill his interleaved texts of Plato's *Republic* and Aristotle's *Ethics* with collations, references, and the philosophy that comes like an inspiration in youth.

A teacher whom Robertson admired was Arnold of Rugby. In earlier days Arnold had been the object of all sorts of abuse; but public opinion swung round in his favor. He came to Oxford to read lectures on modern history. The room appointed was too small; the audience, Robertson among them, moved to the Sheldonian Theatre. Arnold walked up to the rostrum with the dignity of manhood in its full powers. Those who had been his followers when all the world seemed to scorn him felt that the hour of his triumph, and of theirs, had come. Yet more than personal achievement was in Arnold's manly assurance. "Those who saw him then will not soon forget the lesson read to them by his calm, dignified, simple step—a lesson teaching them the utter worthlessness of unpopularity or of popularity as a test of manhood's worth." Robertson remembered the example of Arnold when he, too, came to feel the sting of slander.

Another case of shifting public opinion was Wordsworth. Like Arnold, he had met severe criticism. Robertson loved his poetry. Shelley and Coleridge also appealed to him, but Wordsworth's principles became more and more the undergirding of his inner life. Later in his career, Robertson lectured on the enjoyment of poetry, especially that of Wordsworth. He then recalled the poet's visiting Oxford to accept the degree of D.C.L. The two galleries and the main floor of the Sheldonian Theatre were densely packed. If Arnold appeared to be concentrative energy, Wordsworth was resignation and peace, with the sunset glow of quietude upon his face.

As Wordsworth came forward, three thousand voices began to cheer him. The applause made the rotunda reverberate like the inside of a drum. The sound rose and fell, caught again and died away, once more crashed loudly, and subsided, rippling into silence. No other man of letters had received such acclaim in Oxford. Young men and old thrilled with an emotion of which they were not ashamed. They were glad that the university, at long last, was honoring one whom they loved. But they sensed the unfitness of such loud praise, as if the noise vulgarized the poet. Robertson observed:

"It seemed more natural and desirable to think of him afar off in his simple dales and mountains, the high priest of Nature, weaving in honoured poverty his songs to liberty and truth, than to see him there clad in a scarlet robe and bespattered with applause. Two young men went home together, part of the way in silence, and one only gave expression to the feelings of the other when he quoted those well-known, trite and oft-quoted lines—lines full of deepest truth—"

> The self-approving hour whole worlds outweighs
> Of stupid starers and of loud huzzas:
> And more true joy Marcellus exiled feels
> Than Caesar with a senate at his heels.

Classics, history, and literature were the staples of Robertson's training in Oxford. He also found much excitement over theology. In 1837 higher academic circles rang with alarms of the growing High Church movement. The question turned upon the limit and authority of the Church. Wherever teachers or students in Oxford spoke of religion—in reading parties, on walks, at the commons, or in their rooms—the question was always the same. Did High Church leaders have the right to place worship above instruction, sacraments above preaching, and the tradition of the Fathers above the direct authority of the Bible? Everyone became an advocate. Some argued to uphold High Church doctrine. Others laughed at it. Still others fiercely pounced on the tracts written by the leaders of the movement, Newman the preacher, Keble the poet, and Pusey the theologian.

In a letter Robertson gave his opinion of Oxford's religious climate. "My friends tell me I am on the high road to

Puseyism, loving Plato, and reading Wordsworth. Μὴ γένοιτο! There is something excessively chilling in the donnishness of Oxford, which insinuates its unlovely spirit everywhere—lecture, chapel, pulpit, Union, conversation, retirement—one feels inclined to say, 'Shall I ever love a human being again with anything warmer than a vegetable attachment?'"

Where a religious question was at stake, he was not likely to be indifferent. He studied the tracts of the High Church party, and he heard its spokesmen. He attended St. Mary's Church near his college. There the sweet solemn voice of John Henry Newman fell upon the Sabbath calm at evensong. Using clear yet marvelously impressive language, Newman preached without ornament or flourish. Robertson was deeply impressed by the sermon "On Sin after Baptism." In later years he recalled "the master's tones, gestures, silver voice, and the few faults of his exquisite, pure English"; and he paid tribute to the man who for years "exercised a wondrous influence over the most intelligent young minds in England. . . ."

Yet Robertson was neither charmed out of his beliefs by Newman's four o'clock service at St. Mary's, nor overpowered by the tracts of the High Churchmen. Through all his student days he clung to the Evangelical faith. The men who became known as the Tractarians did not win his support. But they did claim his thought and time. He gathered ammunition for the controversy from Calvin's *Institutes* and Ranke's *History of the Popes*, as well as from many of the countertracts that kept Oxford presses busy in 1838–39. Then, too, he began to see more than ever the necessity for an accurate knowledge of the Bible.

Each morning, while shaving and dressing, he memorized a certain number of New Testament verses. Before he left

Oxford he had twice gone through the King James Version, and once and a half through the Greek. Moreover, he grouped related texts according to doctrine, so that on the spur of the moment he could summon the Biblical evidence for what he believed. His study of the Book of Acts convinced him that, on the subject of baptism at least, the High Church movement had gone astray. Through his study of the Bible and history, he formed an opinion from which he never swerved: Newman and the other Tractarians were pious, earnest, but mistaken men.

Newman did not carry all of Oxford. His strength was with the students; the college heads and tutors strongly opposed him. Mr. Churton, vice-principal of Brasenose and tutor of Robertson, gave his voice to the chorus of dissent. At the close of Robertson's studies at Oxford, the tutor and his student were left alone in the deserted college. Morning and evening of the early summer they paced the quadrangle. The large sundial on the wall marked the hours of their discussion. They explored the foundation of the Tractarian Movement, asking how far the Early Church really held similar views of worship, the sacraments, and authority.

Then came that further question—were such views the right ones to hold? Was the Church of the first three centuries the all-sufficient guide of the Church in England? Why not go to the words of Christ rather than to some allegorical interpretation of His words? Mr. Churton said that he and his student "not only read together Taylor's *Ancient Christianity*, and verified and compared his passages and quotations from the Fathers, but also read several whole treatises from which his extracts were derived." In all this study there was nothing to make Robertson change his point of view.

Writing to his father about the same time, Robertson mentioned "the paralysing effects of this Oxford delusion-heresy." The words of St. Paul to the Galatians, he thought, applied equally to Oxford: "I would that they were cut off which trouble you." His tutor no doubt influenced his beliefs. The next year, when the celebrated Tract Number 90 burst on Oxford, Churton of Brasenose was one of the four tutors who addressed the editor of the series, criticizing High Church doctrine, and calling upon the anonymous author to give his name to the tract. That name, of course, was John Henry Newman.

Not only religious controversy appealed to Robertson's questing mind. He was also interested in debate on national and international affairs. In his first year at Oxford he joined the Union, a mimic Parliament conducted on the model of the House of Commons. The questions that agitated British government brought a corresponding, and often more lively, discussion in the younger House. According to the minutes Robertson once moved " 'that in the administration of the affairs of India by a British legislature, a one-sided toleration has been in effect an intolerance unparalleled in the policy of heathen nations.' The motion was carried."

John Ruskin was a fellow member of the Union. He was a slim young man who dressed in eccentric fashion; his college mates regarded him as "a kind of butt." He was remarkable even then for his sharp tongue, and for his towering alpine sentences that rose, phrase on phrase, to majestic heights. Ruskin had a passion for the dramatic. He loved the theatre. Therefore he moved on the floor of the Union "that Theatrical Representations are upon the whole highly beneficial to the character of the nation." He argued *pro;* Robertson argued *contra.*

At the time of the debate the clergyman, Mr. Davies, was

visiting the Union. He sat with his friend Robertson. Since the young man had addressed the Union only once or twice, he was more than a little nervous. Before he rose to speak, he whispered, "Davies, pray for me!" His words did not exhibit an irresistible power of oratory, whereas his opponent brought into play the tricks and flounces of debate. The rebuttal was cleverly sarcastic. Ruskin had the Union laughing at Robertson. With sly phrasing he hinted at a well-known personality, to whose sway he thought Robertson had given undue prominence. Again Robertson whispered to Mr. Davies: "Why! the man is describing the devil!"

There was much, however, on Robertson's side. If he had a real Puritan distrust of the theatre as it existed then, he was not alone. Few self-respecting citizens of the early nineteenth century disgraced themselves by going to the theatre; and few, very few authors sullied their reputations by writing for the stage. When adultery became a forbidden motif after the decline of the Stuarts, there seemed to be very little left to write about. The result on one hand was tragedy that wore the unfeeling grimace of a death mask; and on the other, the false emotion of the domestic play and tearful comedy. While yet a student Robertson abhorred sentimentality, in the theatre as elsewhere. He argued that to enjoy feelings without acting upon them is moral cowardice. This theme with variations ran through his entire ministry. He first hammered out his convictions in debate.

Before he left the Union, Robertson became its treasurer. On a number of occasions he presided. He gained accuracy in argument, and his mind reached toward new horizons. These were the years of youthful impatience, when he was dazzled with the golden treasury of knowledge. He wanted to grasp everything at once. But he was disappointed. When he came up to Oxford he had expected to discover an ideal world; instead he found that the brilliant made jokes about the lectures. He supposed that no one entered college but men who were prepared and willing to study; instead he heard the loafers using stock answers and evasive replies. Oxford was not the paradise it seemed from a distance.

Robertson did not let disappointment become an excuse for his own laziness; he fagged hard at his reading and debate. Even so, he remembered Oxford with something like regret. He saw what others have seen in the backward glance, that the university had offered him something that he missed —the value of a long-range, definite plan. "The excitement of theological controversy, questions of the day, politics, gleams and flashings of new paths of learning, led me at full speed for three years, modifying my plans perpetually. *Now* I would give 200 pounds a year to have read on a bad plan, chosen for me, but steadily." He blamed himself, not Oxford, for his failure to seize a rich opportunity.

After he had been a minister for several years, Robertson outlined a method of study: work according to a plan; do not aim at too much; do not become too fastidious; and seek what is actual and real, instead of theories or daydreams. He wrote this advice in answer to some questions of a university student. "Mathematics, classics, and theology, are your work for three or four years to come, and I would bend my energies rather upon acquiring these thoroughly than scattering my efforts over a large surface. I well know the discouragement which there is in feeling how little of all that can be known is within our grasp, and the temptation which there is to try a hundred new fields of knowledge. But the man who succeeds in life is, allowing for the proverbial exaggeration, generally the man *unius libri*.

"Life is very short; and the painter must not hope to be a good seaman; nor is the clergyman to pine because he cannot be the man of literature. I would not be anxious about German at all, but put it resolutely aside till my college career should be over. It can be acquired in after life. Hebrew, Italian, and German I learned after leaving the university, and now that I have them, I do not set much value on them. As to French, if you can conveniently spend some months in the country now, in conjunction with your pursuits of other things, I can see no reason why you should not. Only, do not be too anxious about these things. It is surprising how little they tell on the great work of life."

If he could only have gone back! "Oh for ten years of youth back again with the added experience of age!" But that could not be; youth had its irreparable past. When his tutors had urged him to limit his efforts to the books recommended for class honors, Robertson declined. Whether he feared the strain of such work, or whether he did not wish to be bound to a given course, or whether the system of "cram" was not to his liking, he did not care for the isolated goals, the self-important schemes of success, and the little prizes and awards of university life. After reading one of Robertson's essays, a newly appointed tutor sent for him, and urged that he go up for honors; the other tutor, Mr. Churton, joined in the appeal. He admitted to his father, "My resolution was well-nigh broken." The examiners gave him the unusual privilege of waiting an extra day for his decision. When he held firm, they gave him a "fourth class," a high distinction for one who had not taken the honors course.

He thought for himself, and lived quietly in the college halls. Robertson was not popular at the wine-drinking, cigar-smoking, noise-making parties of the undergraduates. But he had a close circle of friends. In his first year he organized a society to discuss the Bible and pray; it lasted for perhaps a year, then died. His Christian fervor had little chance to glow in Oxford. One of his friends remarked that he was "not ashamed of Christ in a place which, though professedly consecrated to His service, offered perhaps more hindrances than helps to a decidedly Christian profession."

The same phenomenon struck Robertson. The university, he declared, was like the contents of a pitcher he had seen that winter: although near the fire, one globe of ice. He was none the less happy to have a few close friends. Mr. Churton, doing duty at the rectory of his brother-in-law, asked Robertson and two other Oxonians to go with him. The family was away; the four men had the house to themselves. Robertson was not the kind of person to ram his way into a group; here, however, he joined freely in the conversation. There were unlooked-for points of common interest. They all agreed that the new surroundings worked a miracle of defossilization; they had left the university as mere acquaintances; they returned as friends.

"Thanks to God, there are a few spirits of a very different cast here! They must be indeed on fire with a heavenly flame to preserve the warmth they do. Two or three of my most intimate and valuable friends especially." Robertson wrote about his companions to his brother overseas. He missed his brother; he had never fully realized how close they had been until he watched the "Sovereign" bear away from the harbor and slip over the horizon. But, he added, "I am getting now a very delightful little circle of friends around me at Oxford, and hope soon not to number among my acquaintance one man whose society I could afford to give up."

One of his friends, a married man, had been reading hard

for a degree. When he failed in his examination, he was bitterly disappointed. Robertson called; his friend was out. The
wife was nearly overpowered with anxiety for her husband.
Robertson could offer only silent sympathy. For some time
he sat waiting for his friend. When the man came in the
house, his wife, hearing his footsteps, suddenly and com-
pletely changed. She held up a brave face; she spoke with a
calm voice. "The hour of weakness was past, and the deep
strong current of a woman's affection bore her up. It was
the reed rising from the storm when the oak was shattered."

Again, writing to his brother during the long vacation, he
said, "I have many friends to me." He had invitations to
spend the summer in several different places—Germany, the
Isle of Wight, Lancashire, London, Cumberland, Malvern,
Islay, Monmouth. But he made up his mind to stay within the
hoary walls of Brasenose, partly to rest after the furor of
the term's end, but more especially for some close reading.
In his letter he described an outing at Blenheim, the oarsmen
of his college stroking their way to the "head of the river,"
the commemoration, the honorary degrees, the prizes, the
poems, the hurried good-wishes and farewells, before parents
and acquaintances asserted their prior claims, and each of
his friends was caught away into the world.

"We all rowed down to Newnham in an eight-oar: the day
lovely. Newnham, the seat of the Archbishop of York, is a
beautiful place, rendered still more so by the many picnic
parties who had gone down, like ourselves, to show the lions
to their lady friends, who, with their light dresses, formed a
lovely contrast to the greensward and sylvan shade. We came
back at night, the plash of our oars keeping regular time to
the more musical strains of the Canadian Boat-Song, and
La Dame Blanche, with which the ladies solaced our toil."

On Friday the nine ladies, and the vice-principal of Brasenose, breakfasted with Robertson. Flowers in silver vases brightened his room. Before each lady there was a delightful bouquet. Since he had the use of the college plate, he admitted that the setting was "gorgeous." After breakfast, then, they rambled through Oxford. "But, alas! the time came for parting, and a melancholy party we were on the last morning: we had been so entirely together. . . . So we shook hands, spoke not a word of sorrow, and I returned to my lonely den, rendered doubly so by the shadowy outline of bright forms and lovely faces, which so lately beamed in it, and still, to fancy, seemed to hover round."

For some time before he took the degree, and a short while after he was graduated, he settled down and read for his ordination in the Anglican Church. He felt as never before the extent of his own ignorance. "I am persuaded that the surest way for a man to be satisfied with his own attainments is to read little; for the more he reads, the more he sees the boundless extent of what there is to be known, and the circumscribed nature of his own attainments. However, perseverance and prayer may do much." Robertson did not count himself to have apprehended; but he pressed toward the mark.

One of his closest boyhood friends, George Moncrieff, was just then beginning his ministerial labors. A few months before Robertson took his examination, he wrote to this friend concerning the years that lay ahead. "The prospect we have, as far as human eye can judge, is a stormy one, and predicts more controversy than edification. It is impossible to look round on the strange aspect of all things—the Church reeling to her centre with conflicting opinions; in all circles,

whether political or religious, minds unsettled and antici-
pating a crisis; 'men's hearts failing them for fear, and for
looking for those things which are coming upon the earth'
—without feeling that our path will be a rugged one, and the
hour of trial is at hand."

III

The Ministry to the Poor

LEAVING college after his examination for the Church, Robertson went immediately to Winchester. In that cathedral city he was ordained. Whether or not Mr. Nicholson, his future rector, knew of Robertson's yearning to enter the army, he preached a sermon on the text, "Endure hardness as a good soldier of Jesus Christ." After the discourse Robertson came before the bishop. He took his vows to assist in the sacraments; to read the Scriptures and homilies of the Church; to examine young people in the catechism; and to care for the poor and sick of the congregation. The bishop laid his hands on the candidate and said: "Take thou authority to administer the duty of a deacon confided to thee in God's Church, in the name of the Father, the Son, and the Holy Ghost. Amen." As the bishop gave Robertson his papers on that midsummer Sunday of 1840, he repeated the text of the ordination sermon. "Endure hardness as a good soldier of Jesus Christ." In his twenty-fourth year, on the threshold of his ministry, Robertson gained a motto for life.

His field of labor comprised three parishes of Winchester. St. Maurice, St. Mary Kalendar, and St. Peter's Colebrook had been a run-down corner of God's Kingdom before Mr.

Nicholson took charge. Nor were they yet ideal. The first of these churches was in the midst of reconstruction; everything but the tower had been torn down. The second formerly had claims to be "the highest rooft pish churche in Europe, ffor by all this tyme yt hath had no other cover but the skyes." The walls had since been demolished. Similarly, the nave of the third church had once enclosed a patch of grass and weeds; but all that remained in Robertson's time were fragments of stonework in a garden wall. Mr. Nicholson, the rector, and Robertson, the curate, had three churches—and they had none! They held services in sanctuaries near by.

Parishioners came from the shabbiest quarter of the town, where men lived in threadbare and anxious poverty, suffered, doubted, and drenched their unhappiness in mugs of ale. As Robertson began his tasks, he quickly forgot university life. The gowns, lectures, and proctors, the august manners and mellow charm of Oxford, were like dreams of another world. Every day his theology rubbed against desperate human needs. Tractarianism faded from his thoughts, and the wonder grew in him that religious men could stress ritual, Church, Virgin—everything, anything but Christ! He had "too much of stern iniquity and hell rampant to grapple with," to give time to the reading of controversy. The three parishes were a battleground of practical faith.

Mr. Nicholson was an excellent overseer of Robertson's work. In the face of strong opposition he was managing to raise a new edifice for the St. Maurice Church. He confronted still more violent antagonism, both from unlettered shopkeepers and from the gentry, in organizing schools for the children of the poor. From a congregation that numbered scarcely a hundred heads, bald and gray, he drew large throngs to the Church, and won the hearts of the people.

What is more unusual, Mr. Nicholson gained the admiration of his curate.

These two men began their work together on the Sunday after the ordination. Mr. Nicholson formally introduced the curate to the teachers of the Sunday school. Robertson took his place in the new surroundings with quiet assurance. He sat by one of the teachers; they talked about methods and problems of instructing young people, and the opportunity of leading boys and girls to Christ. Shortly afterward he spoke to a class of about a dozen big, tough fellows from the neighborhood. He did not have a certain stiffness around the collar that often sets a young minister apart from the rest of mankind. He talked naturally. Leaning forward, he urged the members of the class to live as Christians: "Believe me, there is nothing else worth living for." Thus early he impressed those whom others found hard, if not impossible, to reach. From the first day of his ministry to the last, he was concerned with the spiritual growth of the young.

On the evening of the same day, Robertson preached to the poor folk of the united parishes. The text was from Isaiah 55:1—"Ho, every one that thirsteth, come ye to the waters, and he that hath no money; come ye, buy, and eat." One who heard his first sermon said that it was a fervid announcement of the prophetic words, not read but *preached*, "with an eloquence, confidence of power, and self-possession I have never witnessed in any similar instance." On the next Sunday, and the next, his assurance grew. The deep voice, the restrained gestures, the earnestness of Robertson made a lasting impression. The churchwarden long afterwards remembered him as a fine young man, "quite soldier-looking," who was as fond as the Apostle Paul of military images. Yet during his stay at Winchester, Robertson gave no indications of pulpit genius. His sermons were natural, interesting, and decidedly religious, but he had only the beginnings of the originality and passion, the depth and force of his later ministry.

Since the parish was in good hands, the work prospered. The attention and numbers gradually increased. Mr. Nicholson and Robertson opened two churches at once, in which they exchanged duties. Both were crowded from pulpit to door. The curate said, "We have a lecture in the week, and two adult classes for men and women, the attendance at which increases weekly, and our communicants have been doubled in the last three months. So that amidst much dislike and disgust from the old High Church gentry of the town, many of the common people hear us gladly, and some of the upper classes are beginning to manifest curiosity and interest."

Success, however, did not make Robertson vain. He knew the weight of his responsibility. In that work he was glad to spend himself: "If a man's heart be set to glorify his Lord with the best service his feeble mind and body can offer, there can be nothing comparable to the ministry." He soon came upon the human tangles that taxed his skill and patience. A few months taught him to endure hardness, and to expect much disappointment. Still he called his work the "highest earthly honour," and when one of his friends was ordained to the ministry, he welcomed him "to a participation of its joys and sorrows." For himself, Robertson was supremely glad to be an ambassador of Christ.

As with other young ministers, Robertson learned step by step. The texts of theology had a way of answering the questions that his simple-minded people did not ask. This fact, however, was no reason for letting his books gather dust. He corrected the fault of his Oxford studies by adhering to a strict plan. In reading the works of Jonathan Edwards, for example, his impulse "came to its limit unexhausted." He stuck to his work, and did not spare a day from the parish. He studied the Scriptures in English and Greek, and began to decipher the Hebrew as well. Once more he realized how much he had to learn. The Church in those times did not require much technical knowledge, and the standards for the minister, if not scandalously low, were none too high. Robertson exclaimed: "How much some systematic preparation is needed in our Church! We enter it almost without chart or compass."

A large share of the pastoral work fell to Robertson, not because the rector thought himself too good for lesser ecclesiastic chores, but because Mr. Nicholson was a sick man. In addition to the ordinary tasks of the diaconate, Robertson seems to have taken much of the "surplice duty." Thus he came near to the hearts of the people when they were most responsive. He entered their lives in the dedication of a child at the baptismal font; in the first acceptance of the communion wafer and cup; in the exchange of vows at the marriage altar; and in the last tender rites for the dead, as the mourners wound slowly up the hill at dusk and gathered around an open grave. In these hours he touched others, and others touched him, in mutual confidence that binds pastor and flock together.

Visitation was a regular part of his work. The district in which he called lay nearly in the shadow of the cathedral tower. The old section of the town boasted a wooden colonnade, gabled houses, and the cathedral itself with the exquisite reredos and the hush of its lengthy nave. But picturesqueness concealed near-by hovels, stifling and undrained, hotbeds of typhus, scarlet fever, and cholera. Robertson did his work where there was none to witness or to praise. He entered the dwellings of squalid poverty; he saw the stale discontent of the poor. "With few exceptions," he said, "I have been well received in the worst places." Robertson made himself familiar with the habits and wages of his people; he knew their wretchedness and ignorance, their aches and thirsts, and above all their utter helplessness. In the filthiest byways of Winchester he learned the romance of the ministry.

Slowly the "shudder of inexperience" passed away; he acquired the habit of sympathy, which enabled him to put up with many things that were disgusting, in order to do good. Robertson's pastoral work was indelible on his memory. When he mentioned social conditions he spoke from first-hand knowledge, as in a sermon to a fashionable congregation: "There is a drapery of life which curtains away from us the loathsome parts of existence. You pass down the gay and glittering streets where almost all the forms which present themselves are forms of busy, strong, active humanity. Out of doors in the public thoroughfares you see the holiday of life. There is squalid poverty in the bye-lanes and alleys. There is sickness in the upper chambers. But you do not see that. . . . You cannot count the houses. . . . But the physician and the minister can. They can tell you what there is behind the scenes."

All the devotion that a man gives to his first love, Robertson gave to Winchester. One who knew him there described his early months in the pastorate. Robertson rose early. He ate little breakfast, so as to begin at once on his work. Then he began to study. He specialized on Biblical criticism and Hebrew, though here as elsewhere he read widely. In brief, this was a time of hard reading and parish calling, of silence and self-discipline. "His way of life was most regular and simple. Study all morning; in the afternoon, hard fagging at visitation of the poor, in the closest and dirtiest streets of Winchester; his evenings were spent sometimes alone, but very often with his rector."

Indeed, Mr. Nicholson was more than a supervisor; he was a real companion. Robertson was pleased to write after a few months at Winchester, "My rector is everything I could wish, as a guide and as a friend. His kindness and that of his wife are unbounded." Again he said, "My treatment I only complain of on the score of exuberant kindness. I live almost at Mr. Nicholson's, and we go hand and heart together." The rector was a good man in bad health. He was to die within a few years. Robertson, who had left Winchester, at once posted this letter of sympathy to the widow:

"My dear friend,—I do not hesitate for one moment whether I ought to intrude upon your sadness or not, for we are mourners together. In your most affectionate husband I have lost a friend, and it is my sad privilege to write to you in your bereavement. I was startled and solemnized by hearing who had been taken from us—for I never dreamed that I should be his survivor—and all our happy Sunday evenings, and country walks, and ministerial union, came rushing over my recollection. Oh, what those days were—and what kindness did you both show to me, as a brother and sister and more! After a moment of bitterness, almost the very first thought that rose on my heart was, his work is done, and done well; and I felt roused and invigorated, instead of depressed, by the remembrance that we have a work to do, and the night cometh when no man can work. I cannot look back to all the past without feeling that his memory is a soothing thing to us all, and almost longing that our own course was as fairly run, and all as safe and secure as it is with him."

Except for the friendliness of the Nicholsons and the devotion of the poor, the people of Winchester offered Robertson little social life, and he did not go in search of it. He seldom went out; his life was largely self-contained. As a man of prayer he spent much time alone with God. In keeping with his study habits, he set aside regular hours of prayer. He borrowed strength from devotional books of such different temper as the *Life of Henry Martyn* and Thomas á Kempis' *Imitation of Christ*. He arranged his prayers methodically:

> *Sunday*: Parish; outpouring of the Spirit
> *Monday*: Act of devotion
> *Tuesday*: Spread of the Gospel
> *Wednesday*: Kingdom of Christ
> *Thursday*: Self-denial
> *Friday*: Special confession
> *Saturday*: Intercession

From the burdens that bowed him down, from the hurry and worry and rush of life, from all his perplexities, he came to the hour of prayer; and thus he prayed: "Bring into captivity every thought to the obedience of Christ. Take what I cannot give: My heart, body, thoughts, time, abilities, money, health, strength, nights, days, youth, age, and spend them in Thy service, O my crucified Master, Redeemer, God." After prayer he felt the leading of God's hand. In his own experience there were instances that he could not doubt. He wrote to a friend: "You can have little idea of the temptations in the ministry to despond and let the hands hang down; and the many hours of doubt and difficulty which come upon the soul. And if to these were added the uncertainty, whether the position itself were one in which we had placed ourselves without God's direction, they would be indeed intolerable."

As a matter of self-control, Robertson fasted. His spiritual exercises were after the manner of a Loyola. He did not lacerate his body, to be sure, yet in his diary he charted the steps and stumblings of his inward pilgrimage. He labeled his sins, analyzed his weaknesses, and catalogued the graces of Christian life as he had need of them. His mind and habits altered after he left Winchester. "Communion with God is not to be attained by abstraction and asceticism, but by the development of Christian sympathies. I John 4:12— 'If we love one another, God dwelleth in us, and his love is perfected in us.'" He found discipline to be not severity but firmness, not the punishment of the body but the enlargement of the spirit.

In his mature sermons he preached often against the dangers of unnatural religion. Denial of self for the sake of self-denial, torture simply as torture, hunger as hunger, or sorrow as sorrow—these have no magical efficacy. "It is a great error when men, perceiving that God's natural penalties and hardships strengthen and purify the spirit, think to attain a similar good by forcing such penalties and hardships upon themselves." Robertson was sure that the world gave rise to enough solitariness; it need not be self-inflicted. He faced the Cross everywhere he went; he did not have to go out of his way to find it.

Perhaps because of his austere habits at Winchester, and certainly because of the pace at which he worked, Robertson's health for the second time began to crack. He feared that his life would not be long. "The quick cough, lassitude, emaciation," were dread signs of consumption that had taken other members of his family. Inflammation of the lungs and bronchial tubes increasingly pained him. Mr. Nicholson urged him to rest. The doctors insisted that he give up his work for a while, and go to a climate better suited to his health. They suggested the mountain air of Switzerland. At first Robertson believed that his case was hopeless. He wanted to drive his body until it fell exhausted. But wiser counsel persuaded him that he could recover health; he took a more cheerful view of his illness; and little as he wished to leave Winchester before finishing the customary two years of service, he knew that he must do something to shake off his torpor of body and mind. He therefore set out for Switzerland.

Before crossing the Channel, Robertson finished his examination for priest's orders. The Bishop of Winchester asked the candidate to summarize the work of a deacon. Robertson gave him a theme so pointed in its suggestions that the bishop kept it, and often showed it as a model to future candidates. On the last day of his diaconate Robertson mailed a letter from Farnham to Mr. Nicholson; he confessed that when he first came to Winchester "there had been no experience of the painful truth that the professional opposition to others' sin does not release a minister from the struggle with his own. . . . Tomorrow I am to be irrevocably in outward ritual set apart to the work of God. I would that it were as easy to be separated for ever from the earthliness within." In his first year he had made the perennial discovery of the minister: that in dealing with the problems of others, his biggest problem lay within himself.

On the whole, however, despite lapses, Robertson always

thought of the brief period at Winchester as the best part of his ministry. He was conscious of having developed himself more truly there than in his later charges. He learned the hardships, the limitations, and the steady drain of energy in pastoral work, and yet he knew the rewards of preaching the Gospel of Christ. His career at Winchester was short but happy: he was the friend of Mr. Nicholson and his wife; he was successful, if not spectacular, in preaching; few critics actually bothered him; the plain poor folk looked up to him, listened to him, respected and loved him. A cloud passed over Robertson only toward the end of the year. He thought that he was going to die. Afterwards he said that he had wished for the release of death; and he added that he did not know then how much God had for him to learn before he should be fit to die.

IV

The Ministry to the Wealthy

ON the Continent, traveling by foot, Robertson went through Germany toward Switzerland. He fell in with other wayfarers along the road, and discussed religious problems with them. For several days he kept company with a young Prussian who hated religion; afterwards two Swiss joined them, one an avowed infidel, the other a wavering Christian. "We parted, I fear, without any good done." However uncongenial the company, Robertson's spirits lifted with the bodily exercise. He took delight in the scenery, as well as the traditions of the Rhine valley. At length he came to his destination, the city of Geneva. Having letters of introduction to some of the eminent citizens, he soon found a number of friends. He took part in the religious discussion of the day, and with his quick mind, nimble tongue, and zest for social and religious topics, he charmed those whom he met.

He spoke of religion feelingly. With anyone who faced religious difficulties or harbored doubts, he was a gentle counselor. But with those who mocked Christ, either by denying His goodness or by holding doggedly to some weird doctrine, Robertson lost patience. He believed what he believed; he said what he had to say in no timid manner; and he gave full vent to his indignation. Not until riper manhood did he acquire the dignity of silence in controversy. Some of his religious debating, however, was of the milder sort. One of Robertson's new acquaintances was Cesar Malan, a minister who led an evangelical revival in the Genevan Church, and was expelled for his zeal. Malan was a kindly, soft-spoken person who enjoyed theological table talk. On one occasion, when they were alone, he and Robertson discussed religious "assurance" for nearly two hours. The Swiss divine enjoyed the vigor of the young English clergyman; they arranged to meet again.

On this later visit, Robertson was disappointed to find that there were several others present. The result was that he did not speak so unreservedly as before. Somehow he wished to avoid an argument before a gallery of spectators; in such a case, he said, it was difficult for him to be calm. Each man would unconsciously think of winning a point, or of impressing the bystanders, instead of gaining knowledge of the truth that makes men free. Two make a discussion; more make an exhibition. Robertson therefore would neither fight nor yield. He stood firm; he was not the kind to give ground. Malan cross-questioned him. But he only parried, for he did not wish to give a public display of his most sacred thoughts.

As they talked, the older man prophesied, *"Mon très-cher frère, vous aurez une triste vie et un triste ministère."* A sad life, a sad ministry! Malan spoke more wisely than he knew.

For the time, however, the future looked bright. In Geneva Robertson met the woman he was to marry, Helen Denys. She was the third daughter of Sir George Denys, of Northamptonshire, then equerry to His Royal Highness, the

Duke of Sussex. After a short acquaintance Robertson married her. Since boyhood he had idealized women, whom he regarded more or less as "beings of another order." Once he had been enamored of a Swedish girl, who gave him a lock of hair, lines of her handwriting, a book, and other trifles of affection; he worshiped her only as "a living rainbow, with no further feeling." Perhaps when he married he did not realize that Helen Denys could be less than perfect. If he was soon disenchanted, he still was glad that he had always tried to live up to his chivalric ideal.

The highest of his ideals concerned marriage. He formed these early, and he was always true to them. As a man Robertson was strong enough to work out in real life what once had appealed only to his imagination. He looked back with thankfulness, never afraid to admit that he strove to be among "the pure in heart." Later on he said in one of his lectures: "It is feelings such as these, call them romantic, if you will, which I know, from personal experience, can keep a man all his youth through, before a higher faith has been called into being, from every species of vicious and low indulgence in every shape and form."

Soon after his marriage he returned with his wife to England, and settled near his parents in Cheltenham. His health had improved, yet was such as to force him to give up the curacy at Winchester. For several months he rested; but he went back to his former parish to give a farewell sermon. The church was full; the congregation was appreciative. He was cheered by the affection shown him on his return. There was a choked-up feeling within him as he saw, from the vantage point of time, what his ministry at Winchester had done for the poor. He always tended to undervalue his accomplishments. But now he said: "From what I learnt I have reason to believe that more than I had thought were savingly brought to Christ during my ministry there."

While he rested in Cheltenham, Robertson was hunting for a curacy that would not overburden him; in other words, a place in which he could share all duties. In January of 1842 he wrote a letter of inquiry and advice to a fellow minister: "I am grieved to hear your account of yourself. Take care. Depend upon it, you will gain nothing by a press of steam, as I now acknowledge with bitterness: indeed, I do not expect ever to be worth much again. Can you tell me of a curacy which combines diametrically opposed qualities— sufficiency of stipend and easiness of work? By easiness, I mean half service, that is, I cannot take on any duty single- handed, but must have either a resident rector, or a stipend sufficient to procure regular assistance. I have had a district church mentioned to me. Such a thing would just suit me."

Robertson began his work the next summer in the district church, located on the edge of Cheltenham. The white stone walls of Christchurch, with a lofty tower, stood on an eleva- tion; the town was in the valley below and in the distance was the smooth undulating outline of the Malvern Hills. The sanctuary was new, in Gothic style, and spacious enough for two thousand persons. The congregation was made up largely of the elite. The residents in the near neighborhood were of the wealthier classes. Like the church, their homes were shining new. By certain standards a curacy here would have been an envied position. Yet Robertson was not com- fortable surrounded by all this elegance. The days had passed when the follower of Christ could say, "Silver and gold have I none."

Writing to another churchman, he said: "You tell me

nothing of your work. Mine is far less satisfactory than at Winchester." There were several reasons for his uneasiness. Cheltenham was a resort for the lame and lazy and rich, a pleasure town where a minister as well as everyone else was tempted to fritter away the time. Needless to say, Robertson had better uses for his time than pleasure-hunting or cultural dissipation. As much as possible he avoided the gatherings and speeches. He concentrated on the work to which he was called. The only important events during his stay in Cheltenham were the births of three children, one of whom died, and the death of his last surviving sister. He lived and worked nearly five years at Christchurch, developing his powers as a minister.

It was a time of continued growth. He got up early in the morning, "dedicating the first warm aspirations to God." Nor did he neglect his study. Preparing to teach the books of Samuel, he plunged into Niebuhr's *Rome* and Guizot's work on civilization, as well as volumes of political economy. In Cheltenham he began to evolve his combination of Biblical truth and historical fact, brought to bear on every-day human needs. He followed the events of the day, supplementing his thought with the Roman Catholic historian, Lingard, the ponderous and trustworthy Hallam, and the orations of Burke. The interpretation of the books of Samuel was his own; he did not lean on commentaries as a crutch. Afterwards he worked over the same material into a course of sermons. Meanwhile he was doing groundwork.

Three writers will indicate his interests. He read Carlyle's *Past and Present*, of which he said, "I have gained good and energy from that book." A contemporary poet whom he admired and whose works he read, Alfred Tennyson, was living at the time in Cheltenham. Of the classic writers he seems to have made a habit of Dante, perhaps the artist above all others supreme in style. Robertson wove himself into the sound and movement of the "Inferno," and memorized the whole of it in 1845. He traveled in close company with such thinkers as these, hiving up their wisdom, forming an individual stamp for his own thought, and strengthening himself for the Christian ministry.

There were two services on Sunday at Christchurch. The Rev. Archibald Boyd, the rector, gave the morning sermon. Robertson read the liturgy. As a reader he was simple, impressive, and devout; he went through the lessons and the prayers as one who felt them. In the afternoon Robertson preached; sometimes he had the entire service to himself. He stood erect in the stone pulpit, a youthful figure, rather slim and over middle height. His head was finely proportioned, of Grecian cast, with prominent forehead and dark auburn hair. His lips, when closed, were a thin firm line of resolution, but when he spoke his mouth was marvelously expressive. His voice was rich and deep. Yet the fascination that he had for the afternoon congregation was more than that of graceful appearance and soothing sound. For those who had the ears and hearts to hear, the words of the young minister braced the understanding, kindled the imagination, and moved the will.

Robertson admired the burning eloquence of Mr. Boyd. The rector was something of a pulpit giant. As though drawn by magnetic force, the curate would lean forward in his seat as the morning sermon rose to a climax; when it ended and the calm ensued, he would throw back his head as if to say, "Magnificent!" Somewhere or other almost every strong preacher has come under the influence of another powerful

man of God. For five years in Cheltenham, Robertson had
the privilege of watching and hearing a master craftsman at
his work. But there was a corresponding disadvantage. If
he admired Mr. Boyd, he also despaired of attaining his
standards. It was like living "under the shadow of the al-
mighty." He set a model for himself that he despaired of
making really his own.

Within a few hours after the morning service, Robertson
followed his rector into the pulpit. With the sermon of Mr.
Boyd still ringing in his ears, he began to speak. The discord
jarred him; he was never satisfied. In his preaching at
Winchester he had dashed off his thoughts between breakfast and luncheon on Saturday. But coming into the pulpit
after Mr. Boyd, it was worse than folly to rely on such hasty
creations. Therefore, he gave long, painstaking hours to the
structure of each sermon, as well as to the writing. It was a
hard lesson that he learned—but invaluable. He discovered
early in his ministry that he must not gamble on the inspiration of the moment; he must read, plan, write, tear up,
rewrite, struggle, agonize, pray. Then he would be ready
to preach.

Although Robertson did not think highly of his own sermons, several members of the congregation observed that he
was more than a common preacher. These hearers rated him
at his proper value, before a larger public admired his written works. Mr. Dobson, principal of Cheltenham College,
knew a good sermon from a poor one; he had been subjected
to both kinds. When he heard Robertson, he listened with
surprise that one so young could speak with such power.
"Even at this moment I can see him, then in almost youthful
beauty, raising his hand above his head as he closed his ser-

mon with the words—'The banner of the Cross, without taking up which,' he said, 'no man could be a Christian.' This generation will not look upon his like again."

One person in Cheltenham had taken a dislike to Robertson, through no fault of his, when the curate had just come to Christchurch. Then he heard Robertson on a Sunday afternoon. The prejudice vanished. The hearer said, "I was not merely struck, but startled by the sermon." The thought was clear and bold, enough to jab back-pew sleepers wide awake, and even tempt dull minds to think. For the most part, however, Robertson appealed to the thoughtful members of the congregation. "The passion held in leash, the tremulously earnest tone, the utter forgetfulness of self in his subject, and the abundance of the heart out of which the mouth spake"—all this, and more, made the new friend decide that Robertson was a man whom he must get to know, and whom he must hear at every opportunity.

It is true that Robertson underestimated the value of his Cheltenham ministry. He had done the same in his first pastorate; and through the remainder of his life he was to go on believing that he fell short of the mark. Whatever he said to depreciate the years in Cheltenham, he had many followers there. From the first he swayed minds that had any point of contact with his own. Lay men and women found in him an intelligible spokesman of religion. His brother ministers also respected him. At meetings of the clergy Robertson usually remained silent. But every so often, when some of the brethren got snarled in the exegesis of a text, he would say "a few simple words which shed a flood of new light upon the passage." He was not much given to take the lead in conversation, or to put himself forward. His fellow clergyman none the less recognized his talents, as did the more attentive members of the congregation.

It is also true that he thought much of his preaching obscure to others. The feeling is common with men who live by using words: he had faced so much of his own lack of knowledge and powerlessness in the hard work of acquiring, that his sermons sounded garbled to him. Then, too, he heard the good souls, who gave a confused echo of his thoughts, with quiet hopelessness. But here again he was better than he judged himself. Even when he had crude, untaught minds to deal with, he made his meaning clear. "I well remember," said an acquaintance, "when spending part of a summer holiday with him, how the newly-built church, which stood apart from the village in a park, became more and more frequented every Sunday by goodly farmers and rustic labourers, who listened to him, all eyes and ears, with a pleasant mixture of delight and astonishment. To whatever class he spoke, the language of his sympathies made him intelligible."

But Cheltenham was a difficult place to preach. Two very different kinds of temperament, the supposedly fashionable and the supposedly religious, at times mingled insensibly there, and again stood at swords' points. Some people exclaimed against the sober seriousness of Cheltenham, while others bemoaned its frivolity and worldliness. William Cobbett described the health resort as "a place to which East India plunderers, West India floggers, English tax-gorgers, together with gluttons, drunkards, and debauchees of all descriptions, female as well as male, resort, at the suggestion of silently laughing quacks, in the hope of getting rid of the bodily consequences of their manifold sins and iniquities." At the same time there was an army of prim widows and spinsters, and of elderly gentlemen, who busied themselves with all things cultural, philanthropic, and religious. The Church had invaded society, and in consequence suffered the blight of respectability.

Thus Robertson battled on two fronts. Preaching about the Church, he said: "Here you have sacraments all regular, and consecrated buildings, ministers apostolically ordained, but worldly men come—flaunting, gay, idle persons to stare —is that the house of God?" Equally as bad were those who went up to the church, not to be entertained, but for the purpose of engaging in some Holy War. Systems of theology, contrived by subtle, overanxious minds, clashed loudly in Cheltenham. Among the poor of Winchester Robertson had seldom run afoul of party spirit; he was startled now by the contrast. He saw the Church splitting along multiplex lines of cleavage. Every division stood against all the others. He stood alone.

As a supporter of "Evangelical" belief within the Church of England, he was expected to say harsh things about his High Church brethren. Charity, the greatest virtue, was the one least practiced among religious groups. Robertson was dismayed at the bitterness with which the extremists of his party compounded their fire and brimstone for the destruction of the wicked. "They tell lies in the name of God; others tell them in the name of the devil: that is the only difference." Especially irksome to him was a clique of gossiping women, whose self-appointed mission was to shape the curate's opinions according to their own, and bridle the honesty of his speech. Robertson called these women his "muslin episcopate."

Congealed opinion, cant, and the divorce of words and practice sickened him. He believed that anyone who claimed to be a member of the body of Christ should try to live as such. Often he came upon the individual who had upturned eyes and a mouthful of over-spiritual expressions, yet had scarcely a breath of true religion in him. Some Protestants seemed to say: "Here is the Bible; read it for yourself; but these doctrines, and no other, you must find in it; inquire freely, but at your peril arrive at any other conclusion than this; here is the truth, and here is the Bible to prove it by." Was Christian faith a fetter? A contract? An ultimatum? Or was there still guidance from the Holy Spirit? These questions forced Robertson to take stock of his evangelical beliefs and his ties with the Church.

"As to the Church of England, I am hers, *ex animo*. I do not mean to say that if I had written her baptismal service, I should have exactly expressed myself as she has done; but take her as she is, 'With all thy faults I love thee still.' As to the state of the Evangelical clergy, I think it lamentable. I see sentiment instead of principle, and a miserable, mawkish religion superseding a state which once was healthy. Their adherents I love less than themselves, for they are but the copies of their faults in a larger edition. Like yourself, I stand nearly alone, a theological Ishmael. The Tractarians despise me, and the Evangelicals somewhat loudly express their doubts of me."

Gradually there settled upon him a feeling of loneliness. He had friends, good friends and loyal. Mr. Boyd was a kind man; a doctor was a close acquaintance; another gentleman liked to discuss philosophy with Robertson; still others shared his passion for literature. But there was none whom he could meet on the deepest levels of his thought and feeling; no one to whom he could safely unburden himself on the impulse of confession. Here at Cheltenham was the first terrible realization of the solitariness that was to haunt him the rest of his life—a feeling that had come and gone before, but now had come to stay. In a busy town, engaged in active work, and with people on every side, he was alone.

Of the silent agonizing hours he left little record. He was storing up experience against the sermons of later years, when he preached on "The Loneliness of Christ," "The Sympathy of Christ," "The New Commandment to Love One Another," "The Pre-eminence of Charity," and "Christian Friendship." These and other sermons revealed the measure of his suffering. He knew; he had been caught in the web of loneliness. Robertson felt with piercing conviction that those around him abused the creeds, the articles, and the catechism; he thought that such documents were like the valley of dead men's bones, very many and very dry, until the Spirit of God transformed them "into living and breathing realities." It hurt him that people should gossip and criticize and damn behind the mask of religion. He disliked the thought of being amongst them: not because he lacked courage or depended on others, but because of the intensity of his beliefs and affections.

In 1845, looking inwardly, Robertson girded himself for the battle of life:

"Resolves—To try to learn to be thoroughly poor in spirit, meek and to be ready to be silent when others speak.

"To learn from everyone.

"To try to feel my own insignificance.

"To believe in myself, and the powers with which I am intrusted.

"To try to make conversation more useful, and therefore to store my mind with fact, yet to be on guard against a wish to shine.

"To try to despise the principle of the day, 'every man his own trumpeter'; and to feel it a degradation to speak of my own doings, as a poor braggart.

"To endeavour to get over the adulterous-generation-habit of seeking a sign . . .

"To speak less of self, and think less.

"To aim at more concentration of thought.

"To try to overcome castle-building.

"To be systematic in visiting; and to make myself master of some system of questions for ascertaining the state of the poor.

"To listen to conscience, instead of, as Pilate did, to intellect.

"To try to fix attention on Christ rather than on the doctrines of Christ.

"To preserve inviolable secrecy on all secrets committed to me, especially on any confidential communication of spiritual perplexities.

"To take deep interest in the difficulties of others so communicated.

"To perform rigorously the examen of conscience.

"To try to fix my thoughts in prayer, without distraction.

"To contend, one by one, against evil thoughts.

"To watch over a growing habit of uncharitable judgment."

In the following year he preached on "The Human Race Typified by the Man of Sorrows." Drawing from the prophecy of Isaiah, he pictured the Christ who was "acquainted with grief." The sermon was characteristic of Robertson in every way: in subject matter, arrangement, mood, and style. In the first place, it was about Christ. He stressed both His deity and humanity—the Son of God who

likewise called Himself the Son of Man. The important fact
to keep in mind, Robertson said, is that members of the human race *can understand* the sorrow of Christ, in kind if not
in degree. Two of his strongest sermons, the ones on loneliness and sympathy, also centered in Christ. He usually
spoke more of Christ's person than of Christ's work, but he
always brought his thinking to terms with his Saviour.
Goodness, Purity, and Truth had meaning because of the
One in whom these were incarnate. The person of Christ was
the very pulse-beat of Robertson's public ministry, as of his
personal faith.

His theology did not hover in the realm of speculation.
He brought it to earth and applied it to everyday living in
Cheltenham. In other words, he did not separate doctrine
and ethics. The sermon about the Man of Sorrows was on
behalf of the hospital, where the poor of Cheltenham came in
sickness. The direct appeal was to the Christian conscience
rather than the Christian purse. Robertson was brimful of
that uneconomic feeling called charity.

"Have we ever looked at the poor man's cottage, and pictured to ourselves how that almost den, small and comfort-
less as it is, can become the sick room of the invalid? There
is no securing repose, for all the domestic work of the family
must be done within a few feet of the bed. The noise of
footsteps entering and retiring goes on all day long, scarcely
divided by a thin partition from the sick man's ear. . . .
Look at consumption in the cottage. Through the perpetually opening door, and through the broken window, and
through the unguarded chimney the death-draughts pour
down hour by hour upon the sufferer, till the fell and painful
malady has done its work, and the rough wretched coffin lies
prematurely on the bed. The damp strikes through the brick

and the mud floor, till rheumatism has stiffened the joints
into contracted uselessness for life. Water from the pond
is often all they have to wet the lips of the dying. There is
not always one free from work to perpetually wet those hot
lips. There is no fire in the bedchamber. Fuel costs too much,
therefore to produce an artificial heat in the depth of winter,
every aperture must be closed and pasted up, and so in the
stifling unwholesome warmth of an overheated cell which
takes away the very breath on entering, human life is gasped
away."

With such words Robertson brought home to many a heart
the pathetic needs of the time. The sermon about Christ and
the human race was a model of careful work, and was not at
all unworthy of the preacher's best in years to come. He no
longer showed fleeting signs of promise. His sermons were
now full-bodied and mature. He did not give the impression
of becoming, so much as of having arrived. The elements of
strength lay partly in the emotional heat of the minister,
partly in the force and simplicity of his words, and partly
also in the mood of sincerity which no man is able to counter-
feit. Under these lay compact, sinewy structure. "The Human Race Typified by the Man of Sorrows" had typically
Robertsonian form. There were two main points, which he
announced at the end of the introduction:

I. *The lot of humanity in this world.* This is the portrait
of the species—"a man of sorrows and acquainted with
grief."

II. *The treatment which depressed humanity commonly
experiences*: "we hid, as it were, our faces from Him."

Mr. Boyd, the rector of Christchurch, was fond of the
two-point sermon; he taught his curate much in the art of
sermon construction. The older man had published a volume

on the doctrines and practices of the Church of England. In three of his four sermons he used the principle of balance. Robertson adopted this method, developed it, made it characteristically his own, and by his example finally spread it to the ends of the English-speaking world.

The Cheltenham ministry brought a crisis in Robertson's thinking. He had made up his mind once and for all to enter the ministry; he had finished his training; he had passed the test of action among the poor at Winchester; he had become an expert preacher at Cheltenham: now, with most of the difficulties seemingly out of the way, he met disaster. The end of Robertson's ministry in Cheltenham, though outwardly uneventful, proved to be the fiercest storm-struggle of his soul. He no longer wanted to be a minister. He was not at all certain what he believed or disbelieved. Doubts came; then remorse for his doubts; and finally despair.

Supposedly he was an Evangelical. But he was ill at ease within the party. He acknowledged the good work done by the better of his co-workers, especially their industrious philanthropy in Negro emancipation, prison reform, missionary work, and the spread of clean literature and national education. He could not mark the exact changes of his thought; but at length he came to believe that his position was false. For a man to accept the dogma of a church or creed or party is a simple thing; to be sure of God in his inmost soul is a different question. Assurance had become the touchstone of Evangelical thought. But with Robertson everything seemed to be shifting; nothing was secure.

Recoiling from Evangelicalism, he examined the system of doctrine on which he had based his life. There were questions in which he found no bottom. He puzzled over the difference between historical and saving faith, asking if it were necessary to have "an impetuous and tumultuous feeling of reconciliation" with God. If so, he was lost. Then came a shock—the rupture of a friendship he thought sealed for life—which shattered his spirits. His health broke again. For a time all was dark. The conflict between faith and doubt, between hope and despair, was in bitterness of soul. One after another his beliefs began to quake and give way, as if he stood on a cliff that was crumbling into the sea.

Afterward he spoke of the anguished hours in which he found his way back to God, struggling out of darkness, and in the end experiencing the sympathy of Christ: "Can you say that He could not enter into our worst sorrows, or that His trials were in 'show'? Comprehend that heart, containing all that was manliest and all that was most womanly. Think what you will, but do not mistake Him, or else you will lose the one great certainty to which, in the midst of darkest doubt, I never ceased to cling—the entire symmetry and loveliness, and the unequalled nobleness of the humanity of the Son of Man. Ask me any questions you will on this, for if there have been a subject I have pondered over and believed in, it is the mind and heart of Jesus."

His body was sick—but more than that. Life itself was sick within him. Once again, on the advice of a doctor, Robertson set out for the Continent. Mrs. Robertson did not go with him; she stayed in England with the children.

V

The Valley of Indecision

ROBERTSON went directly to the Tyrol by way of Munich, and then to the mountain regions around Innsbruck. Later he traveled to Switzerland, and finally to Heidelberg. The majesty of the hills seized upon him. His letters pictured the changeless yet ever-changing mountains, at times thrusting upward into the gray coolness of the clouds, again flashing silver in the blaze of the sun, or shading from rich purple to black with the coming night. Continually in his later sermons and lectures he lifted up his eyes to those hills where he had found his help:

"Go where the strong foundations of the earth lie around you in their massive majesty, and mountain after mountain rears its snow to heaven in a giant chain, and then, when this bursts upon you for the first time in life, there is that peculiar feeling which we call, in common language, the enlargement of ideas. But when we are told that the sublimity of those dizzy heights is but a nameless speck in comparison with the globe of which they form the girdle; and when we pass on to think of that globe itself as a minute spot in the mighty system to which it belongs, so that our world might be annihilated and its loss would not be felt; and when we are told that eighty millions of such systems roll in the world of space, to which our own system again is as nothing

. . . then, brethren, the awe which comes upon the heart is only, after all, a tribute to a *portion* of God's greatness."

In the Tyrol he carried on his silent, inward, lonely struggle of the soul. The stages of the conflict are uncertain; but they are also unimportant. The fact is that Robertson always looked back to this time as one of hard-fought decision. It is enough to know that he wrestled, like Jacob, until he received a blessing. Who was Christ? What is inspiration? What are miracles? Is resurrection fact or myth? What saves a man, and how? Is there individual life hereafter, or only a gassy "consciousness of the universe"? On the human plane he saw things darkly. "After finding littleness where I expected nobleness, and impurity where I thought there was spotlessness, again and again I despaired of the unreality of goodness." His one last human hope collapsed. He doubted that right and wrong made any difference.

Even so, he kept striving as he doubted, and clung to the moral wholesomeness that he suspected was nothing more than a will-o'-the-wisp. There were doubts, but none of the moanings after the fashion of some mid-century poets, nor upbraidings of the God who, according to these men, possibly did not exist at all. When Robertson had come seemingly to the end of everything—the end of hope, the end of faith, the end of all that he had trusted in and believed—then moral duty steadied him. Of one thing he still was sure. No matter what else was right or wrong, he never doubted that Christ was good.

By the time he reached Heidelberg he had gotten his bearings. There he found minds that could understand him, if they could not help. He had release from his doubts, for he could express them. "I have conversed much and freely on the points of difficulty." Robertson met well-informed, agreeable folk in the English chapel, which he supplied for six weeks during the absence of the chaplain. One of these persons was Henry Crabb Robinson, forty years his senior, who like most cheerful old people enjoyed the company of the young. Seated at the same table-d'hôte, they plunged into a discussion of German literature, at which Robertson had been working. They agreed on a walk together the next day.

The elderly man made notes in his diary concerning his new friend. "He is liberal in his opinions; and though he is alarmed by the Puseyites, he seems to dislike the Evangelicals much more. I like him much." Crabb Robinson went to the English chapel, a room in the museum, where he heard Robertson preach. He thought the sermon admirable, "much too good to be thrown away on a congregation of forty or fifty persons." Moreover, it was effective. The minister alluded to the sufferings of the Irish and the poverty of countless Englishmen. Robinson noted in his diary: "I was led to give twice what I intended."

At first, however, preaching was secondary. Robertson was on the Continent to improve his health. The cure-all in those times seems to have been robust exercise, even for one who was at the limit of his endurance, on the theory that if he lived through the activity he would also pull through the illness. For example: he and a Tyrolese jäger stayed in the hills, and got up at half-past four one morning to try for a shot at a chamois. They walked all day with no game in sight. Robertson described the hunt: the stars, the mountain sunrise, and "the clouds curling beneath us and wreathing themselves into fantastic forms as if the morning light were torturing them." He did not get a chamois; but he said that he was more than repaid by views that not many Englishmen had seen.

Robertson exercised almost furiously. One incident shows his doggedness. On a walking tour of the Tyrol mountains, he planned a leg of the journey that everyone said was impossible. He hired a man to carry his knapsack, and at a little after five o'clock the two men set out on the road. The morning sky was clear, but snow had fallen in the night, and the path was slippery. Before long his guide was "done up"; so that Robertson lifted the knapsack to his own shoulders. Long hours of tramping blistered his feet. In one descent he sprained his ankle. Still he plodded on for twenty-six miles of mountain walking. He was utterly scornful of pain.

Mountain scenery in all its variant colors and moods excited him, but he was disappointed with the character of the mountain people. "I have found less simplicity, less politeness, and far less cleanliness than I expected. Religious they certainly are, if crosses and virgins almost at every quarter of a mile be a proof of religion." There was a chapel beyond every other turn in the road; at each inn he found "holy-water" in his bedroom; and usually in the dining hall there was the likeness of the Saviour. But these had little effect: the people gambled, smoked, drank, and talked in a way that Robertson thought woefully at odds with the presence of Christ.

"And this I believe is the very essence of superstition—to feel great reverence for certain objects, visible or invisible, on account of some mysterious influence with which they are supposed to be endowed, but an influence which all the while has not necessarily any moral effect or any connection with character." His opinion of the Tyrolese went down the more he saw of them. They were "hospitable, simple, honest," to be sure, but "only so long as they have no temptation to be otherwise." This trait followed superstition. Anyone who crouched before a crucifix, said endless prayers, and looked on worship as a charm, and who yet refused to humble himself before God, was a coward. Robertson did not observe much rugged Christian character in the Tyrol.

During his travels he wrote descriptions of nature, his thoughts about places and people, and the inner moods that colored his outward vision. The following extracts are from letters that Robertson addressed to one person, his wife.

"From Munich to Innsbruck I travelled with a young Frenchman and two Italians, the one a cardinal and the other apparently his secretary. These two spoke neither French nor German. We were much struck by seeing them for nearly an hour occupied in prayers from their breviaries. It seemed as if it would never be over. But the way in which they did it was exactly that of a schoolboy humming over his lessons. They corrected one another when a mistake was made, smiled, took snuff, opened the windows, shut them down, had a few words of conversation now and then by way of interlude—reminding me very strongly how inevitable a tendency there is in all forms, even the best, to lose all the spirit which once animated them, and become like lifeless corpses. No doubt those prayers were once the expression of true and fervid feeling. Now, a very cardinal can scarcely go through them without yawning.

"For a stage or two from Munich the country was perfectly flat; but at length it began to put on the features of mountain scenery, till at Partenkirch it became really grand. . . . In all this glory there is a strange tumult in my bosom for which I cannot assign any cause. Grandeur makes me misanthropic, and soft beauty makes my heart beat with a misery that I cannot describe. . . . After my arrival at Innsbruck I wandered alone by the gush of that wild and roaring river. Everything was still and solemn. Mighty shadows were moving silently across the valley, like so many giant spectres, as the sun went down behind the hills. The outlines of the mountains gradually blended in a sky which became by degrees as black as themselves, and I was left in the grandeur of darkness. I felt, as I generally do on such occasions, strongly, the swift rush of time—on and on, bearing everything along with it into the Infinite; and here are we, for a moment powerless nothings, but endued with powers of agony and thought which none but immortals feel. Then I went slowly back to Innsbruck, heard the hum of life again, saw the windows glittering with light, heard the drone of the church bells, and met the crowds coming away from vespers. It all seemed a dream."

"The pass of Ampezzo, the shortest between Innsbruck and Venice, is remarkably wild and noble. The shape of the mountains, as well as their height, adds to this grandeur. They are peaked, serrated, and jagged in all directions. After the somewhat tiresome, because unaltering, scenery through which I had gone, this sudden view brought new sensations, and sent the blood thrilling to the heart, and then running about in all directions, not knowing where to go. After getting about half through, it came on to rain, a drenching shower, for two hours. But this scarcely diminished the beauty of the scene, for gleams of sunshine every now and then revealed unseen peaks through the rain, and the clouds drifting in masses round the peaks, now dipping down, and now leaving all bare, formed a picture exceedingly striking."

"I am now writing in the stove-room, public room or whatever it is to be called, the only sitting-room in the cottage, surrounded by shepherds who have come in wet through, and are discussing their supper and their sour wine—a new scene of life; but I am more at home with them than in Cheltenham. My guide is supping with me—an honest modest Italian—on some dish whose composition I cannot guess, and dare not ask."

"I have just finished a letter to you, but still I must begin another, that I may put down my impressions while they are fresh. For I feel strongly that, in this world, things can be felt but once; you cannot recall impressions. You recall only part of them, softened and altered, bearing the same relation to the impression itself that the mellowed Italian does to the original Latin. Pictures, scenery, persons, you can feel them in this world but once. The first time never returns. . . . I closed my last letter at Corfara, after getting in drenched and half frozen to a miserable little inn, resorted to by the shepherds when their day's work is done. Twenty or more sat at tables round me, redolent of garlic, sheep, and tobacco. I make it a duty to feel myself at home in every society—so I pushed half my supper across to one of them, to his evident surprise, and afterwards spread out my map, when the whole party crowded round us, and I delighted them by pointing out to each his native valley or village."

"You cannot conceive how England is detested throughout Germany. The *Allgemeine Zeitung*, the leading newspaper is perpetually attacking us—our behaviour in India, our religious hypocrisy, our slavery to forms and fashions, our commercial policy, etc. A short time ago the *Times* had, in some article, remarked upon the great advantage derived by Germany from the English travellers who pass through it. Upon which the *Zeitung* replied, that if a few innkeepers rejoiced at this, the whole nation mourned. 'Only let God deliver us from the affliction of that horrid nation passing through our towns and besetting us like a plague of flies in our diligences, hotels, walks, with their stupid faces, their vulgarity, their everlasting inquisitiveness about hotels and sight-seeing, and utter inability to appreciate anything higher, and it would be a day of jubilee for all Germany.' I do not give the words, but that was the purport of the article."

"Here I am again [at Innsbruck], my pedestrian excursion being over. And now, to take up the thread where it last broke off. I had reached the top of the Stelvio, just after wading ankle deep through snow and slush, up the most wonderful road in Europe. As usual, I did it fast, accomplishing in six hours and a half what a man in the hotel-book boasted to have done in nine; nay, four miles more—for he started from Prad, and I had a full hour's work to get to Prad. When I got to the very summit, faint with exertion, the clouds hid the grand view from me. . . . I went back next morning so far as to try my chance again, through snow which had fallen in the night as deep as my knee, and on drifts deeper than the hip. But a grand sight awaited me at the top: the sun shining on the magnificent Orteler Spitze, whose peak of snow glittered in brilliant contrast to the bare bleak rocks of his sides, down which, as if in streams, his glaciers, glittering brightly too, descended into the valley. I had a curious series of manoeuvres to get rid of an oily, stupid Italian. What a relief it was!

"I cannot tell you how the love of solitude has grown upon me. I can enjoy these mountains, with their sombre pine woods and their wild sights and sounds, only when I am alone. Rocks and crags crumbling down in a long line of ruin; uprooted trees hurled headlong, bark and branches gone, and their black stumps dotting the mountain far above, where they were before the avalanche or the torrent reached them; wild birds soaring and shrieking as you pass along, disturbed perhaps from their feast on a dead horse; the clouds sailing solemnly in long white lines above, or wreathing themselves like living shrouds round the crags. There is grandeur and wonder in all these things; but the spell is broken if human beings are near you."

"I have taken my path through Switzerland, and pass to-day, Sunday, here [in Schaffhausen]. The hotel is about two miles from the town, and is just opposite the Falls of the Rhine. . . . The weather has once more become warm and lovely, so different from the bleak weather I had in the Tyrol. . . . The well-known form of the Jungfrau cuts into the clear sky, white and sharp, with that peculiar outline which you only see in this clear atmosphere—looking indeed, as if there were no intermediate atmosphere. Last night I sat up long in my bed-room, unable to get to sleep, watching the Fall of the Rhine by moonlight. The pale beams fell beautifully on the white foam, making the dark rocks darker still by contrast. The spray rose up, floating like thinnest silver tissue; and the incessant roar of the falling water, softened by the distance into a murmur like that of a forest shaking in the wind, might have served for a soldier's dirge or a poet's lullaby. It was singularly solemn: stars silent and clear above, looking out of a sky of infinite blue; no wind, no cloud; and the stone statues on the terrace below . . . glittering cold and white, like spectres, gazing on the convulsion of the Rhine beneath them.

"An English family and myself are alone in this great hotel, yet I have not offered to perform the service for them. I cannot. Even to read prayers seems an effort beyond my power. More and more I feel that I am not a minister, and never can be one."

Exercise had failed in its work of restoration. Robertson was more tired at the end of his walking journey than at the start. From the first he had difficulty in getting to sleep. When asleep, melancholy brooded over his slumber. One night he mentioned as an example: he dreamed that someone was gossiping to him about his friends; they all were sad because he was trying to deceive his people with husks; his sermons were empty, meaningless. He woke—then slept—and dreamed again. This time he was brought to task for duties left undone: words unsaid, children untaught, sick unvisited, with names of which he had never heard, all in the convincing grotesque of dreams. Night after night was the same. He rose before sunup "to drive away the spectres," though sleeping or waking made slight difference. He had no rest. The day had one advantage; he was able to put some thoughts out of his mind. "But directly I sleep, the power of banishment is gone. I sleep but little; yet that is no gain, for my half-waking dreams are worst."

Change of scene had done no good, conversation with men of foreign lands had not cheered him, and bodily exercise had profited little. When at last he came to Heidelberg, he had to think definitely about his plans for the future. He resolved to give up the curacy at Christchurch. He had been too free in expressing himself there, for which his wife reprimanded him. He told her by mail: "You were perfectly right. I was most unwise to bare my feelings even to the extent I did. A man who 'wears his heart on his sleeve' must not be surprised if he finds it a temptation 'for daws to peck at.' That I said as much as I did to any human being, I now deeply regret. But I shall go on doing so to the end of the chapter." And yet his outspoken words concerned only himself! He had "babbled out truths"—simple truths he thought, almost childlike—which others could not understand in Robertson.

Sympathy was so exquisite a gift that he could not resist the desire to have it for his own. He learned that people who sympathized in sickness, bereavement, or some other misfortune, often drew an iron curtain around themselves when it came to religious perplexities. That was Robertson's experience. He would make someone his confidant, who would assume an air of shocked innocence, twist his words, and perhaps repeat them. There would follow a "fit of misanthropy." But his mood never lasted, and then, he said, "that absurd human heart with which I live trusts and confides again—and so I go on, alternately rich and bankrupt in feeling. Yet, yet, say what I will—when any one soothes me with the semblance of sympathy—I cannot for the life of me help baring my whole bosom in gratitude and trust. A very expensive, perhaps a generous, but certainly a very weak way of giving lessons in anatomy gratis—vivisection performed by the lecturer upon himself." He decided that he must take his own course, ask for no advice, and expect sympathy from no one.

Cheltenham still was his home, but he felt like a stranger there. He had made up his mind to leave Christchurch. When he began his walking tour he had thought of forsaking the ministry as well. Yet he could not. "To give it up seems throwing away the only opportunity of doing good in this short life that is now available to me." Believing that he would die early, Robertson wanted to spend himself in worth-while endeavor. To continue as he was promised further wretchedness. He spoke once more of his sermons, "perpetually bewildering people," and his words that did not say the thing he meant. Moreover, he had gone through a period of questioning. Could he hold up the light for other men to see, when doubts swirled darkly in his own mind?

Preaching worked a transformation. When Robertson occupied the pulpit in the Heidelberg chapel, he had a grip on himself. He knew that his place was in the Church. The question was: Where? Two or three plans occurred to him. "The only one I shall mention at present, as the one that I think I shall try first, is not to give up the ministry, but to make the experiment of working in a country parish, in which I have to deal with the poor only." For some reason he felt that he did not have the right sort of natural equipment as a minister to the rich. Perhaps his manner or language grated on them. His thoughts were not their thoughts. Furthermore, he could not help being angered by men who put the entrance fee to heaven in pounds sterling. He was more at home with the rightful heirs of the Kingdom, the poor in spirit.

While making his decision he preached every Sunday in Heidelberg. "I have had more proofs of my ministry telling here than during my whole stay in Cheltenham. . . . I have been much tried by the unexpected warmth with which the congregation here have testified their regard at my departure." Two persons told him that it would quench their spiritual life if he should leave. A French gentleman coaxed and argued. A woman wept. Robertson wrote to his wife: "I may say it to you, the request that I should remain has been unanimous. And yet I feel, in looking over the past, that all this bright sky would be clouded over once more, excited hope would end in failure." His absence from England was not altogether a religious waste, he said, but the congregation at Heidelberg had overrated his ability as a minister.

Those whom he had drawn around him belonged to the classes he thought himself unable to teach. "Then to feel estrangement again, to see suspicion awaken, misunderstanding arise, and to give up another congregation in bitterness, would be too much to bear." However strongly he wished to stay, he made plans for returning to England. The church people would not give up hope; they insisted that he should not leave them. Robertson was uncertain. "Is this a call from God or not?" The members of the church wanted him because of his preaching; individuals because of his understanding mind and compassionate heart. They did not wish to be left stranded. If Robertson were to stay in Germany, however, he would lose touch with the work in England. The salary in Heidelberg was meager, and even though the cost of living was less there than in an English town, Robertson had to think of providing food and clothes for his wife, his children, and himself. "Now balance all these things together," he wrote to Mrs. Robertson, "and tell me what you think, and also what my father thinks." From them, and from them only, he was willing to take advice.

After an absence of nearly three months Robertson went back to Cheltenham. He was less improved in health than his friends expected, though far more tranquil in mind. He had given up the curacy of Christchurch. As health came back he sought a new field of labor, but he said, "If I take work, it must be single-handed. I am afraid I can no longer brook to walk in leading-strings." He found a parish in St. Ebbe's, Oxford. It was not an easy post. The church was in the least desirable part of town, the parishioners had been neglected, and the salary was miserably small. After two months, he was asked to fill the vacancy of Mr. Kennaway, who had left Trinity Chapel, Brighton. He refused. It would be an unmanly failure of duty to leave Oxford. But the bishop thought otherwise, the trustees of the chapel made their offer once again, and in the summer of 1847 Robertson came to Brighton. He was thirty-one years of age.

VI

The Town of Vanity Fair

ON the chalk cliffs of southeastern England, its face toward the blue sea, and the green downs behind its back, Brighton spread its establishments over a three-mile front. In mid-nineteenth century there was perhaps no more famous resort in the land. There were all the standard attractions of a watering place: an assembly hall, a band, a theatre, and a library. Brighton added what then were novelties, an esplanade, and pier from which to view sky, ocean, and waves whitening on the beach. The more fashionable places rose east and west along the cliff. Away from the shore were the second- and third-rate houses, with their cramped rooms, lumpy beds, tough meat, and stale cabbage. Brighton was a typical seaside resort.

To the casual eye everything was gay and brilliant. Yet near the center of the town sprawled a section called "The Lanes," mustily ancient in odor and construction, which Brighton had hemmed in and tried to forget in back of stylish buildings. Dwellings for the poor also squatted on the outskirts of Brighton. The town had its darker side; it hid its poverty as something indecent. But it turned a bright façade to the sea. The buildings and streets, the dress and manner and entertainments of the people, all gave evidence of wealth and pleasure. The resort was known throughout England for its "wind, glare, and fashion."

The population of seventy thousand was fluctuating and varied, as changeful as the tides on the pebbly beach. Something like one-fourth of the people were transients. The numbers swelled on the week ends, as the train rattled down from London on Saturday night. In addition to the pleasure hunters from the city, there was a vast residential population. Among the citizens were army officers and civil servants retired from active life, gentlemen of leisure, and elderly businessmen who had won their fortunes elsewhere. The city of Brighton was newly developed and overcrowded. Robertson arrived there in August; he had difficulty in finding a place for his family to live. After a tedious search he made arrangements to move into 9 Montpelier Terrace.

On August 9, 1847, he wrote from Brighton: "At last I am able to tell you that we have fixed upon a house—the above being the address—into which we hope to move to-morrow. . . . I can form no conception yet of how I shall like my work. Brighton is too large to have the disagreeable peculiarities of Cheltenham; and Kennaway's congregation seems to be chiefly composed of tradesmen. That will relieve me from much that I expected of unpleasantness. Still, looking at the many disadvantages there are, I have great misgivings as to that kind of success which a proprietary-chapel needs—the filling of seats, etc. But Brighton seems a healthy place, and I am sure it is bracing. My wife is decidedly better than in Cheltenham; and the heir to my estates and title spends hours on the beach tossing stones into the sea, without speculating about their future destinies, or the probable depth of the ocean into which they fall."

That week the family settled in their new surroundings. The following Sunday, August 15, Frederick W. Robertson of Brighton preached his first sermon in the Trinity Chapel. For the text he chose, "The Jews require a sign, and the Greeks seek after wisdom, but we preach Christ crucified." Some praised the sermon, and others criticized. But all sensed that there was a new voice in Brighton, manly, urgent, and prophetic. In the first months his success was gradual. Acclimated to the soft ways of the former pastor, a High Churchman, many who attended the chapel were stunned at the manner of preaching. Some left; more came. The young minister did not have long to fret over the demands of a proprietary chapel, "the filling of seats, etc." He never had to waste his eloquence on empty pews. In fact, the problem was quite the opposite.

As the autumn tide of visitors flowed down from London, and the season rose to its height, the question was how to accommodate all who wished to hear the new preacher in Brighton. He attracted all sorts of people, and especially the men. He was admired by men of science and culture, and by rough-handed artisans; by ladies of title, and by domestic servants; by men of staunch faith, and by others who possessed hardly a shred of religion. A few ministers in Brighton addressed larger congregations, but none moved such varied types. Robertson preached to them all, until the worshipers thronged the sanctuary from the pulpit stairs to the gallery, and the dingy, squat chapel of brick and mortar became a place of pilgrimage.

There were other churches, of course, and other ministers. At this time the Anglican churches in Brighton numbered thirteen and the Dissenters' nineteen, along with a Friends' Meeting-house, a Jewish Synagogue, and a Roman Catholic church. Among other pulpit figures in the town, one of the most widely known was the Rev. Joseph Sortain. Notwithstanding a thin wire of a voice, he preached well. The numbers who listened to him at Huntingdon Chapel were larger than those at Trinity; over one thousand of the elite turned out each Sunday "to hear Sortain." A countess thrilled at his eloquence: "How new, how clever!" A shoemaker had his own views; he preferred Robertson: "Just compare him with a man like Sortain. Sortain would be twenty minutes in finding fine pegs to hang his words on." But the words of Robertson, he said, haunted his steps for days.

In October of the first year, Henry Crabb Robinson visited Brighton. He soon found the young minister who had impressed him at Heidelberg. In his diary he noted that Robertson was already popular, and had stirred all who came to hear him. The new minister had driven some High Church ladies from the congregation, but no men. "On Sunday I heard Mr. Robertson preach, and I was very much pleased with him. He has raised quite a religious tumult here. He is fully aware that his liberalism will make him many enemies; but he ought to rely upon it that for every enemy so raised he will gain two friends."

The next Sunday Crabb Robinson turned again to the chapel. "Who would credit such a thing of me? I heard three sermons last Sunday!!! I went in the evening to hear Sortain. In the morning and afternoon I stood in the gallery of Robertson's church. The morning discourse was one of the best I ever heard. . . . It was delivered without any apparent note, and was full of striking thought." The afternoon lecture he did not rank so highly, and therefore advised Robertson to follow a manuscript. The older man saw in the younger "no abatement of his cordiality," and incidentally no change in his preaching habits.

During these first months at Trinity Chapel, Robertson acquainted himself with the people of the church. The tradesmen were a source of strength to their minister. They were the kind of folk who made Robertson glad to be an Englishman. Their homes were clean, their shops tidy, and they sold good wares. For well over twenty-five years the tradesmen had taken thoughtful interest in politics and social reform. They found a sympathetic leader in Robertson. The professional classes, too, came to hear him preach. In his sermons he used illustrations from the experience of the physician and surgeon, the lawyer and teacher, the engineer and architect, the students of chemistry, physics, astronomy, and other branches of science. Finally, he attracted the people of wealth or title who could see beyond the little circle of social affairs. These worshipers in Trinity Chapel gave Robertson courage to speak God's message to his generation. The people of Brighton affected his preaching as much as his preaching affected the people of Brighton.

As a gathering place for amusement, however, Brighton had a fascination for other sorts. On the promenades the minister walked by crowds of fashionable idlers. In his chapel he spoke to many of them. He often preached on such themes as worldliness, the illusiveness of life, or sensual and spiritual excitement. There were other matters with which he had to deal, but the one constantly overwhelming problem was Brighton itself:

> The weight of meanness, selfish cares,
> Coarse manners, vulgar passions, that beat in
> On all sides from the ordinary world.

After dark the theatres drew large crowds. The ballrooms were filled. Billiard rooms sounded with the click of balls and the noise of laughter. The drinking places for the well-to-do were jammed, while the gin palaces did a thriving trade among the poor. Nights became days of pleasure in Brighton. Robertson revolted from the light-footed, light-headed gaiety.

At seven o'clock in the morning the walks and broad avenues were empty. A few invalids crept toward the "spa" before nine. But as the sun warmed the central promenade, called the Steyne, then ladies and gentlemen—young and old—on foot, on horseback, and in carriages, began to swarm along the rim of the cliff. From then on everything was movement, in and out, coming and going. An article in *Punch* (attributed to Thackeray) sketched a pen portrait of Brighton in this year of 1847:

"The cabs, the flys, the shandryshans, the sedan-chairs with the poor old invalids inside; the old maids', the dowagers' chariots, out of which you see countenances scarcely less death-like, the stupendous cabs, out of which the whiskered heroes of the gallant Onety-oneth look down on us people on foot; the hacks mounted by young ladies from the equestrian schools, by whose sides the riding-masters canter confidently—the crowd, Sir, on the Cliff was perfectly frightful. It is my belief that nobody goes abroad any more. Everybody is at Brighton."

These birds of feather flocked to Brighton in the autumn, stayed for a season, and then took flight back to London. Robertson pondered what he saw: faces that were self-indulgent and at the same time hard. "It is wondrously instructive, as we pass through the crowded town, to see each face except the very young, careworn, and having lines of suffering; and we are tempted to ask, Where are the happy ones?" A rhymester set the passing scene in doggerel:

> Alack! to see their stupid stare
>   As down the Steyne they take,
> Like things with broadcloth souls, the fair,
>   As fair as paint can make.

If other authors, such as Cobbett, Macaulay, and Dickens lampooned Brighton, there was truth enough to justify their satire; and if Robertson preached against the worldliness of the place, he did not choose the topic. It thrust itself upon him. Trinity Chapel stood on Ship Street, almost at the center of dazzling Brighton. Near at hand were the theatre, the music hall, the promenade, and the ornate Pavilion. Robertson felt the contrast between his work and the hubbub around him. For what he called the "world chase" he had only pity. "It is the spirit of worldliness," he declared, "which makes a man love show, splendour, rank, title, and sensual enjoyments; and occupies his attention, chiefly or entirely, with conversations respecting merely passing events, and passing acquaintances." If instead of "worldliness" he had said "Brighton," he could not have hit upon a better description.

Robertson did his best to knife through this crust of worldliness. The old complaint at Cheltenham redoubled its force; he could never tolerate "those who are familiar with all that you can tell them of misery, and still go on feasting, and dressing, and amusing themselves, and doling out the driblets of their income with a grudge in the sacred cause of benevolence." The outward show and the inward wretchedness of the crowds clashed together. Robertson's message to

Brighton at the end of his ministry, as at the beginning, was this: "Measure all by the Cross. Do you want success? The Cross is failure. Do you want a name? The Cross is infamy. Is it to be gay and happy that you live? The Cross is pain and sharpness. Do you live that the will of God may be done —in you and by you, in life and death? Then, and only then, the spirit of the Cross is in you."

Even though he had scarcely begun his work at Trinity Chapel, Robertson was already tired. He was too much in earnest to ask for rest. His nerves were tensely strung, his mind toilworn, his body exhausted. Brighton levied a dreadful tax upon him. Then came sorrow. He was away in London when Mrs. Robertson gave birth to a child. But the baby died. The mother was haggard, and her heart was heavy, but Dr. Taylor said that she was recovering. On November 29, 1847, Robertson addressed a letter to a friend:

"I only write you one line to tell you of a sad loss and disappointment we have just sustained. My wife has been prematurely confined, and the little girl, a perfectly beautiful thing, is dead. I have just returned from putting my little beautiful one myself into her grave, after a last look at her calm, placid countenance lying in her coffin. It was by starlight, with only the sexton present; but it was more congenial to my heart to bury her so than in the midst of a crowd in the glaring daylight, with a service gabbled over her. In the infinite expanse of darkness there was more of heaven and more of God, to my soul at least, and more of that deep, still rest, more profound than death, of which death is but a shadow, for which we are all craving, and in the depths of which we shall soon be—how soon!"

Brighton—fashionable Brighton that is—was jesting,

drinking, dancing as usual that night, adding fuel to the fever of excitement. But by a small open grave Robertson looked up to the stars, keeping their silent watch over the earth, and in the heavens he saw an emblem of the deep repose of God.

VII

The Spokesman for Laborers

THE Books of Samuel speak of the clash of mighty men. They are dramatic; still they do not appear to be revolutionary tracts. In January of 1848, however, Robertson had begun an exposition of the first book, and was feeling the ice and fire of religious indignation. He told of Samuel as a prophet, Saul as a king, David as the Lord's anointed. He seldom made direct mention of current political events. He took for granted that basic human problems do not alter from age to age. When some of his listeners objected to his teaching, he answered that he was not to blame if the truths of First Samuel fitted more periods than one. The people were not blind; they saw the parallel. He talked of government; he dealt with the rights of a sovereign, of a wealthy person, of a laborer; he spoke much of the brotherhood of man. Fighting words in the year 1848!

Those very problems troubled England. Through the winter the clouds of discontent grew menacing. Across the Channel the shout of "Liberty, Equality, Fraternity" was in the air. Lamartine declared France a republic. There were revolutions throughout the Continent. The workmen of England began to stir up social questions, and made new demands on their government. In March of 1848 there were demonstrations in London, Glasgow, Edinburgh, Liverpool, and other cities; the Chartists threatened to imitate the February revolution of that year in France. Robertson did not want civil war. None the less, he took hope in the signs of the times. In a letter he said: "The world has become a new one since we met. To my mind, it is full of hope, even to bursting. I wonder what you think of these tumults:

> For all the past of time reveals
> A bridal dawn of thunder-peals,
> Wherever thought hath wedded fact.

Some outlines of the kingdom of Christ begin to glimmer, albeit very faintly, and far off, perhaps, by many, many centuries."

Strangely, the Church had not been complaining of a gangrened social order. Robertson was one of the few brave men to speak out concerning the issue. He thought of Jesus looking on human injustice, "face to face, and front to front"; and like Him, "he met it, rebuked it, and defied it." His eyes were sharp: what he saw of evil, he denounced with the fury of a prophet; what he saw of good he praised. Loving England's ancient virtues, he detested her ancient wrongs. But he was no radical. He believed in the Established Church, in England, in the Crown and Empire; in the brotherhood of all men within a benevolent aristocracy; in a good God governing the universe. Nor was he reactionary. Robertson did not wail for the past. He was forward-looking, optimistic. Otherwise he could not have declared in the uproar of 1848—"There are better times coming."

A number of Brightonians, on the other hand, did not share Robertson's prophetic zeal. The do-nothings asked why government and business should not continue as in the past hundred years. The strongest appeals left them still assured that the old way of doing things, with all its short-comings, was natural and necessary. Robertson could not agree. He looked for change, and believed in progress. The people were astonished at his doctrine, and many were scandalized at his use of the Bible. In church they did not want politics, however expository and Biblical. The murmurs among a few aristocrats boiled into open complaint, "that they should not be so taught in the presence of their servants and inferiors." The never-ending buzz was almost too much for the young pastor. Friends advised him to leave the chapel. For a while he was tempted to fill out his year, and then look for another pulpit. He stayed in Brighton, how-ever, until the end of his life.

Trinity Chapel had drawbacks. Robertson confessed that his work was "full of encouragement, but full of a far larger amount of misunderstanding and dislike than I had expected to meet with"; and he said, "I work alone with 'many ad-versaries,' and few to bless; but with a very distinct convic-tion that I am doing something." Tongues wagged. He tried to hold his own, without explanation, apology, or argument. Was he to answer petty charges one by one? He would let his character speak for itself. But someone addressed the bishop, anonymously, of course, protesting against one of Robertson's "political" sermons. This action forced the preacher to defend himself and his message.

Accordingly Robertson sent the bishop a copy of the ser-mon, described his method, and answered one who had made a serious charge against him. In the first place, he had said nothing to call for episcopal censure. Moreover, he had always thought and often said that a clergyman had no business meddling in partisan politics, except as a private citizen casting a ballot. In conclusion he made the statement: "I feel that in dealing with God's truth a minister of Christ is clear from the charges of presumption if he speak strongly, yet affectionately, of evil or faults in his social superiors. It brings no pleasure with it. It makes him personal enemies. It is ruin to his worldly interests. And worse than all to a sensitive heart, it makes coldness where there was cordiality. Yet through life I am ready to bear this if need be. An earnest searching ministry among the rich is very, very saddening work. The rest of my life will be consecrated to the poor."

Within the year he was able to befriend the poor of Brighton. The times were anxious in England, above all in the history of the working classes. The old system was breaking up; the new had not yet emerged. There was much unrest. Custom, law, and financial interests stood in the way of social reform. Scattered voices in the Church (for example, Frederick Denison Maurice and Charles Kingsley) demanded justice for the poor. For the most part, however, chapel stewards and local preachers were cautious-minded, soft-mouthed, of good standing in their chosen circles, but hardly the stuff of which prophets are made. "The Great Unwashed" needed a champion. Robertson, with courageous breadth of heart, did not hesitate to speak of "my friends— the working classes."

The chance to help the poor came in a roundabout way. Early in the year Robertson made a pastoral call on Mr. Herbert Holtham, a member of the so-called upper classes. Mr. Holtham was ill. On his sickbed he had time to think. The sermons of Robertson lingered in his thoughts, and he decided that he could not run away from his obligation to the poor. While he lay in bed one question kept hammering in his mind: What could he do to help the working men of Brighton? Something was needed over and above the alms and soup and leathery buns, the ragged blankets and castoff clothing, that went by the name of charity. There was some higher duty than to sustain life hardly worth the living. Though some doubted it, the poor man had a mind and soul as well as a body. Mr. Holtham was convinced that there ought to be a reading room and library for the poor of the town. He told his idea to Robertson; they made plans together.

To be sure, the idea of a reading room was not original with Mr. Holtham or his pastor. The London Working Men's Association sought to improve its members with reading and debate; and there were hundreds of satellite groups in the provinces of England. Brighton itself had libraries, but the doors were shut to the artisan whose hands might be dirty. The very poorest workman had a place in Mr. Holtham's scheme—the man whose education, if anything, had been a few scrambled lessons of reading, writing, arithmetic, and nothing more. There was no free library, and no other open door inviting him to make good his scanty gains. He had as much right to books, newspapers, and journals, as to the public streets and parks. But no one seemed to care about giving a poor man his rights. Mr. Holtham therefore saw his chance to befriend the workers of Brighton.

Robertson believed in the plan. So did the workers. More than one thousand men joined. Each promised to subscribe a penny a week to the funds. With their money they secured a house on Middle Street, and being workmen, they cleaned and papered it themselves. Some books they purchased; others they accepted as gifts. But the library, the furniture, and the building they were proud to claim as their own achieve-

ment. They also took pride in the fact that they could man-
age their own affairs. Robertson did not wish to interfere.
Before the opening of the house, he sat with one of the com-
mittees. The gathering pleased and a little surprised him.
With one or two exceptions the men who spoke were plain
hand laborers. He did not hear oratory, but something that
he thought far better—"straight-forward, honest, English,
manly common sense." That night as he went home along the
dark streets his steps were lighter. If her men were like that,
there was hope for England.

Lady Henley, the youngest sister of Sir Robert Peel, was
among those friends whom Robertson interested in the plan.
He wrote to her: "I am anxious to enlist your sympathy in
the cause which I am trying to assist. The case is this. About
1,000 working-men in this town have just organised themselves into an association which, by a small weekly subscrip-
tion, enables them to have a library and reading room. Their
proceedings hitherto have been marked by singular judgment
and caution, except in one point—that they have unex-
pectedly applied to me to give them an opening address." He
went on to express his concern that there be no suspicion or
coldness on the part of those who ought to help. It was no
trivial matter. In talking with the workers he had become
increasingly aware "of an amount of bitterness and jealousy,
and hatred of things as they are, which I had not before
suspected in its full extent. And people go on saying, 'Peace,
peace, when there is no peace!'"

As for the opening address, Robertson was doubtful that
he was the man for it. He had recently excused himself from
lecturing to the Athenaeum, on the plea of ill health. Furthermore, he had been a resident of Brighton little more than

a year, he was a young minister, and he thought himself "without name, without influence, without authority, without talent" for the address on this particular occasion. Some older person would command more respect. Yet the workmen did not despise his youth; they insisted that he give the speech. Robertson could not snub the invitation of the men who represented more than a thousand of their fellow workers. As a minister of the Church of England he felt bound to accept.

His office was the ministry of reconciliation, "a link of union between the two extremes of society." He firmly yet respectfully demanded that the wealthy pay their debts to the poor. But his sword cut both ways. He wished "to soften down the asperities and to soothe the burning jealousies which are too often found rankling in the minds of those, who, from a position full of wretchedness, look up with almost excusable bitterness on such as are surrounded with earthly comforts." With these thoughts he consented to make the speech. If he did not have a surplus of energy, he would give what he had to help the workmen.

Monday, October 23, 1848, was the evening of the address. Although he did not have much time to prepare the outline, the words hit their mark. He stressed the need for education. Political ignorance was national suicide. An English ecclesiastic of the time said that the people had nothing to do with the laws but obey them. Robertson, however, declared: "If there be a man in the country to whom politics are of personal consequence, it is the labouring man. . . . If an unfair tax be imposed, a man in the upper ranks will scarcely be compelled to retrench a luxury in his establishment; but to the poor man it is almost a matter of life and death. There-

fore a labouring man will be, must be, a politician; he cannot
help it: and the question is, whether he shall be an informed
one or an uninformed one."

Sailing close to the wind, Robertson never swung into a
position that favored a special group. His simple thesis was
that good government exists only because of good citizens,
whether rich, poor, or in between. Facing him at that moment
were men of every hue in the political spectrum. The Tories
wanted to demand strict loyalty to the Crown. The Conservatives wanted to keep "things as they are." The Whigs
and Radicals wanted to throw the entire cargo of tradition
overboard. The Chartists wanted to establish universal manhood suffrage. What if any one of these parties had its desire? Would there not still be the threat of a tyrant on the
throne, stagnation in Parliament, anarchy throughout the
realm, or a many-headed majority as corrupt and misguided
as the clique swept from power? Above all else, England
needed men of staunch character.

"You explain this moral improvement," said Robertson,
"to be 'the elevation of the habits of the working man.' " If
better times were coming, they would not be the magic result
of changed governmental institutions. There must be a
change in men. If England were on the highroad to destruction, the fault would be in lax moral fiber. Egypt, Greece,
and Rome had fallen; Spain, Venice, and Holland had been
shorn of strength. England's fate might be as theirs. "But
one thing is certain, that the decay in morals in all these
cases preceded the decay of institutions." Robertson therefore believed that in an attempt to supply moral vigor, the
Working Men's Institute had "begun at the right end."

There would have been no beginning at all, he reminded his

audience, had it not been for the good will of the upper classes. "You have asked for sympathy. I say that you have it." Strange point and new! He gave credit to the wealthy. They were not all oppressors. While they had not done their whole duty, they had already done much, and were eager to do more. "Who have busied themselves in insuring for the labouring man better ventilation, personal and domestic cleanliness? Who are they that, session after session, fought the battle of the working man to abridge his hours of labour? Who, after long and patient investigation, brought before the country the hideous particulars of women labouring harnessed in the mines, and children young in years but gray-headed in depravity? A band of English gentlemen, at the head of whom was one who has surrounded the name of Ashley [Lord Shaftesbury] with a glory, in comparison with which the concentrated lustre of all the coronets and crowns in Europe is a tinselled gewgaw, and which will burn brightly when they have passed into nothingness."

Undergirding his speech was Robertson's theory of inequality. He accepted the fact that human life has an above and a below. Some persons have more natural advantages than others. In his address to the workmen, he talked bluntly of a "lower" and an "upper" class. At another time and place he said that the constitution of the world was not democratic but aristocratic, not presbyterian but episcopal: "Make all men of equal rank today, and tomorrow there will be found those who have acquired influence over the others." He appealed, then, for a new order. Not birth, not wealth, not learning should be the standards, but goodness, charity, and wisdom. There should be less bowing to riches and title, and more genuine respect for character. In Robertson's eyes a cobbler was as much an heir of God as a king. He looked forward to a spiritual equality, in those better times when *merit should find its own level*.

A newspaper correspondent took shorthand notes of the address. He gave the transcript to Robertson before the living thought was frozen in print; there was no rewriting. A review in the *Christian Reformer* welcomed this new voice in Brighton "as one of the ablest and most eloquent clerical advocates of popular education that it has been our fortune to meet with." George Moncrieff saw a copy of the speech, and congratulated his friend. But Robertson found that it was his role as a celebrity to be "a good butt for rotten eggs and cabbage stalks." He said of the address: "It has attracted more notice than it deserved, and than I expected, vituperative and laudatory; has been read by her Majesty; distributed by nobles and Quakers; sneered at by Conservatives; praised by Tories; slanged by Radicals, and swallowed, with wry faces, by Chartists. But I do not mean to notice any attacks upon it. It is very faulty; but I know that it has done good. I only wish that I had done it in a less hasty way."

In his pulpit Robertson brought the Gospel light to bear upon the world in which he lived. Thinking of immediate problems, he constantly appealed to the future. He knew that the world was on the eve of titanic change, more vast than anyone dared imagine. What that coming day would be, none could tell. Some looked for an era of abundance and peace; others, warfare and convulsion. Meanwhile Robertson had the tongue to express "the dim, vague longing, the restless tossing" of his age. He preached the Gospel to the poor, healing to the brokenhearted, deliverance to the captives, light to the blind, and liberty to the crushed. For him 1848 was "the acceptable year of the Lord."

VIII

The Loneliness of the Pastor

ROBERTSON was a lonely man. The isolation that began in 1847 and 1848 grew more painful in 1849. "More and more, day by day," he wrote to Moncrieff, "one's soul feels itself alone with God, and resolved to listen for His voice alone in the deeps of the spirit." Moncrieff was as close a friend as Robertson ever had. As schoolboys they had played at prisoner's base as if there were no such thing as sorrow. But Robertson could not ignore the fact that the friends of his boyhood were not those of his later years. As life went on, he was growing away from the friends of his youth, and none could fill their places. Memory invaded his loneliness. Events long past came before him as if they were yesterday, and his mind, unbidden, recalled the unforgotten years of boyhood. Of a school friend he said:

"He is gone—with all his fresh, bright, marvellous flow of happiness. What is there more to be said than is contained in those dreadful words—He is gone? How often I have thought of the evening he left Tours, when, in our boyish friendship, we set our little silver watches exactly together, and made a compact to look at the moon exactly at the same moment that night, and think of each other! I do not remember a single hour in life since then which I would have arrested, and said, Let this stay. And to William all was so bright and hopeful!

"Why should we wish him to have remained a little longer? —to have been slashed or mangled . . . and then be lost among the names of the innumerable gallant hearts that are made clay of to satisfy the cupidity of East India merchants? Oh no! better, surely, as it is. And as to the eternal question. We know of him—what is all that we can ever know of any one removed beyond the veil which shelters the unseen from the pryings of curiosity—that he is in the hands of the Wise and Loving. Spirit has mingled with spirit. A child, more or less erring, has gone home. Unloved by his Father? Believe it who may, that will not I."

The old familiar faces were already going—or gone. None of the new acquaintances in Brighton entered so deeply into his life. All the while he gave the impression of an independent and fearless temper, quietly resolute, above human frailties. Was not such character proof against loneliness?

The story has oozed out that even his wife mistook him. She saw his genius over the breakfast table, and that was too close a range. Apparently she was not concerned with her husband's work, and did not share his expectations for the ministry. Sometimes, not often, he mentioned Mrs. Robertson in his letters. At best the picture is a sketchy outline: there are glimpses of her in the home at Montpelier Terrace, arranging a bouquet of flowers, pouring tea, or entertaining an unexpected guest at dinner; waiting for the preacher in the vestry at the close of the afternoon service; and in a later year, smoothing the pillow for her husband in his illness. It may be that he seldom talked of her because, as he said of a friendship, "Every year I feel less inclined than I once was to get upon subjects of the deepest interest. Every year I feel that utterance profanes feeling, and makes it commonplace." It is more likely, however, that she never fathomed his mind, and was unable to sympathize with what she could not understand. Even under his own roof, and perhaps there most of all, he had lonely hours.

Frequently in his letters Robertson mentioned the solitude of the Brighton ministry. Mingling in society he considered largely waste motion. In 1849 he and Mrs. Robertson dined out occasionally. They went to one dinner party of ten or twelve persons. "Conversation after, chiefly military, turning on Indian battles; so I talked." And another time: "A pleasant party enough; that is, there were a good many intelligent men, and the conversation was of a better order than usual." But even so he was glad to have "escaped at 9.20." Sometimes he entered into the conversations, but for the most part he was content to remain in silence, listening to the commonplace chatter, or else to draw out the awkward fellow in the corner who suffered from neglect. Unless he was sure of a friendly hearing, he did not broadcast his views in society. He was constantly with people, and constantly alone.

Some Brightonians had a flair for argument, and were always sniffing to catch the scent of the heretic. Robertson heard "sundry warnings" in private and "pregnant hints" in public. On all his work there lay an overcast of suspicion and mistrust. He did not meet his critics with faltering statements or wriggling excuses. Even had he so desired, he could not have satisfied all of Brighton's hundred jarring creeds. When he spoke in public, his tone was decisive. Each sermon he began, not as a traveler asking for the safe route, or inquiring after the opinions held by "respectable men," but as a pioneer who thrusts out to find his way alone. He disturbed those who never pushed their thoughts to a conclusion, and also the ones who would not listen to a conclusion other than their own. As a result he heard their shrill criticism.

Charges hit Robertson from all quarters: he got accusations in the mail; he got them through the journals and the local newspapers; he got them in the vestry, on the street, and from visitors in his home. A woman called one day at Montpelier Terrace. She spied the *Memoirs* of William Ellery Channing, the Unitarian, on the drawing-room table. She was horror-struck at a minister's taking poison. "I am sorry to see you read this book, Mr. Robertson," she said in a frosty tone. He explained that he never cringed from false doctrine. "I am not so sensitively afraid of error as that. I throw myself on the Father of lights, read all, and trust that He will answer a desire for light." He added that if either of them reached heaven, they would find Dr. Channing there— "which she has, no doubt, duly reported to the Brighton inquisition for heretics."

Despite all criticism, Robertson knew that in a sense he was popular. Indeed, there was such a blaze of popularity that it annoyed him. As a college student he had written to his mother, "I do believe the station of a popular preacher is one of the greatest trials on earth." Experience had not caused him to change his mind. He wished now for honest eloquence; that is, skill to express the right thing, at the right time, in the right way. But he hated blare and bluster, and he called mere fluency the "fatal gift." He had little use for those orators who tried to speak better than they were able. Nor did he like to be classed with such men. Facile tongues and easily won reputations for saintliness irritated him. He would not be taken for a popular preacher; and he would not accept a compliment if he thought that it was given on a misunderstanding of his real intention.

While Robertson could make phrases sparkle, he did not practice tricks of gesture or sleight-of-tongue. "Eloquence, rhetoric, impressive discourses, etc., etc., etc.,—soft gliding swallows, and noisy impudent tomtits—is the true worth of the first orator in the world. I believe I could have become an orator, had I chosen to take the pains. I see what rhetoric does, and what it seems to do, and I thoroughly despise it. I think it makes people worse instead of better; exposes the feelings to tension, like the pulling constantly of a spring back, until the spring loses its elasticity, becomes weak, or breaks; and yet, perhaps, I do it injustice: with an unworldly noble love to give it reality, what might it not do?" Church-goers thought that they flattered him when they called him an orator, a "popular preacher." Such praise was the one thing he least desired.

Filling the role of a popular preacher vexed him to the end of his ministry, and put a sharper edge to his loneliness. At one time he said: "I wish I did not hate preaching so much, but the degradation of being a Brighton preacher is almost intolerable. 'I cannot dig, to beg I am ashamed'; but I think there is not a hard-working artisan whose work does not seem to me a worthier and higher being than myself. I do not depreciate spiritual work—I hold it higher than secular; all I say and feel is, that by the change of times the pulpit has lost its place. . . . Nor am I speaking of the ministerial office; but only the 'stump orator' portion of it—and that I cannot but hold to be thoroughly despicable."

Again he exclaimed: "Would to God I were not a mere pepper-cruet to give relish to the palates of Brightonians!"

Sermons were like a sprinkling of cayenne. He imagined how a cook at one of the Brighton hotels must feel in catering to the appetites of fussy London ladies. "If you knew how sick at heart I am with the whole work of parlement, talkee, palaver, or whatever else it is called; how lightly I hold the 'gift of gab'; how grand and divine the realm of silence appears to me in comparison; how humiliated and degraded to the dust I have felt, in perceiving myself quietly taken by gods and men for the popular preacher of a fashionable watering place; how slight the power seems to me to be given by it of winning souls; and how sternly I have kept my tongue from saying a syllable or a sentence, in pulpit or on platform, because it was popular!"

Like all earnest souls who try to follow a plan of God in their lives, Robertson had his hours of disappointment. Sunday night and all day Monday, after the exhaustion of two thirty- or forty-minute sermons, moody thoughts drifted in like fog from the sea. What troubled him was not so much the things that he had done and said as the things he had neglected to say and do. The law of boundless duty was written upon his heart. Yesterday had gone; its lost opportunities would never come back. He had the corroding sensation that life was short, strength limited, and he had a gigantic work to do: "Evil put down—God's Church purified—good men encouraged—doubting men directed—a country to be saved—time going—life a dream—eternity long—one chance, and but one forever." The odds seemed overwhelming in this solitary struggle of the soul.

Outwardly he was successful, but the thought of a hidden failure haunted him. As he looked at the throngs each Sunday, he could not help wondering how many had come, not from spiritual yearning, but from habit, or curiosity, or an urge to peck at flaws. At times he grew sick to think that he had won local fame, and to some extent captured the hearts of the crowd, but done "very little in the way of gaining souls." No thought could have been more bitter.

He put his whole heart into every sermon. Yet how many routine worshipers did he jar from their set ways, or even stir? Robertson preached with all his might. The organ breathed its benediction on the people. Friend linked arm with friend, remarked on the sermon, and turning away from the pulpit, talked of hats, horses, and the prospects of good weather. "Another Sunday done: crowded congregations, pulpit steps even full, ante-room nearly so. Morning, the Sabbath subject; the afternoon, the conclusion of Acts xviii. I sat in church thinking, 'Now, how this crowd would give many men pleasure, flatter their hearts with vanity, or fill them with honest joy! How strange that it is given to one who cannot enjoy it, who takes no pains to keep it, who would gladly give all up, and feels himself in the midst of all a homeless and heartless stranger.' "

He was alone—yet not alone. For there were two words always in Robertson's mind and on his tongue. One was loneliness; the other was sympathy. The first was the ailment, and the second was the cure. If he did not persuade everyone who heard him, there was comfort in knowing that he touched many others at the point of their deepest need. He knew men and women as individuals, one by one. All sorts of people attended Trinity Chapel, and afterward found their way to Montpelier Terrace to see Robertson. A laborer spread before him the problems of the Working Men's Institute; an elderly woman brought him her spiritual questions; and an English gentleman came with a book of philosophy tucked under his arm. His day was punctuated by visits from the bitter, the angry, the perplexed, the brokenhearted and lonely. He listened to each story, and accepted every burden as if it were his own. The drain on his spiritual reserves was incessant; but Robertson had a huge capacity for suffering with others.

He tried earnestly, if not always successfully, to come near to every human soul in a "wondering, inquiring way." This was by no means a simple thing for Robertson. He was by nature militant and impulsive; there was in him something of pride and self-will, held in tight rein. For all his abundant sympathy, Robertson was an austere man, intensely proud. He disliked compliments and resented criticism. The fatuous approval of seat holders, whose fees supported Trinity Chapel, hurt and humiliated him. On the other hand he felt the sting of critical tongues. He was acutely sensitive. In his earlier days he had not been altogether free of intolerance, and even in Brighton, when deeply moved, he could be irritable, impetuous, and outspoken. But he learned that in giving sympathy to others he gained mastery over himself.

After a woman had stated the shallowest thoughts in the broadest manner, during a long, sluggish visit, Robertson remembered Christ's way of dealing with the individual, and then thought of his own: "I do believe that there ought to be more interest in humanity and more power of throwing one's self into the mind of every one, so that no visit should appear dull. An infinite being comes before us with a whole eternity wrapt up in his mind and soul, and we proceed to classify him, put a label upon him, as we should upon a jar, saying, 'This is rice, that is jelly, and this is pomatum,' and then we think we have saved ourselves the necessity of taking off the cover; whereas, in truth, the Tory, Radical, Evangelical, gossip, flirt, or featherbrain are all new beings in the world:

such a one never having existed before, each having a soul as distinct in its peculiarities from all other souls as his or her face is from all other faces."

Sympathy, his rule for pastoral work, became the habit of his soul. He gauged success neither by the numbers who heard him, nor by the applause of a larger public. Instead he looked for changed lives, and waited for confessions of those in whom a newborn faith had found welcome lodging. This came by the individual touch of sympathy, rather than by speaking loud or long. He had the shepherd heart. "Visit," he said: "do not relieve, do not advise." Often help was needless and advice an insult; a handclasp said more than words or money. He went in and out among the people, and his overcharged heart, longing for companionship, found relief as he ministered to troubled souls.

There were times when he complained of his own laxity in pastoral calling, for he did not make the rounds so often as he wished. Quite naturally he gave preference to the bereaved and the sick. "My visits among the poor to-day included two very sad cases. One, that of a poor family, the father of which is just dead, and the mother a hard-working worthy woman overwhelmed with grief, and crushed by inability to pay the funeral expenses. Only £4! And to think that £4, lavished like pence by tens of thousands of the wealthy people in this country, can make eight or nine human beings free, and the want of it reduce them nearly to starvation. I was able to promise to defray the bill—not all out of my own pocket; the gratitude and relief were touching indeed.

"The other case was that of a poor creature, whom I left with what appeared an abscess in the cheek-bone. It is now pronounced cancer. The pain amounts to agony, incessant and intolerable. Morphine stupefies for a short time, and chloride of lime partly purifies the horrors of the mouth; but in that state now for months she must remain, and no earthly power can save her, scarcely any even assuage her torture." From the hour of that visit, he said, he could not bear to laugh: "I have been thinking lately much, sadly, self-condemningly." He resolved to do his pastoral work, and do it well, but he was never able to say, "It is all done." His body might wear itself out going from door to door; there was no exhausting his sympathy.

A visit from Robertson was an event. Sometimes in his calls on the poor he asked a friend to go with him. More often he went alone. He looked like a soldier, walking with quick step, shoulders square, his body wrapped in a military cloak. Yet his manner was not such as to frighten the poor; he did not wear the grim holiness that makes other men awkward in its presence. He listened to the little domestic tragedies of the poor housewife, the gripes and ailments of her husband, and the ramblings of even the dullest child. The pastor sensed the tongue-tied sorrow of the washwoman whose husband was a drunkard, and remarked that there was "plenty of unwritten poetry lost among the soapsuds." In short, he was touched with the infirmities of the poor. When Robertson made a visit, he was welcome. And the chair in which he sat became a family prize.

Robertson also ministered to the gentlefolk of Brighton. He knew the city at its opposite extremes. He possessed the true culture that knows how to act in any surroundings. He climbed rickety stairs to the lodging with one sleeping room, two beds, and a family of nine; and he entered the spacious drawing room with its oil paintings and hand-carved furniture. He spoke with equal courtesy to the woman at her tub and to the prim aristocrat. His circle of acquaintance in

Brighton included some of the foremost citizens. He was a frequent visitor in the Horace Smith home, a rendezvous of intellectual society. Among his friends of culture he numbered Lady Henley, Lady Lovelace, and the wife of the poet, Lady Byron, who unsealed her life story to Robertson, and told him the secrets of her marriage and separation. Sometimes the barrier of etiquette made the people with money or title unusually hard to reach. But they too had their problems.

For example, unbelief was common. French skepticism had begun to infect England. German vivisection of the Bible was spreading its gloom. Criticism was proving that everything was wrong, even the critics. Therefore, some thought that a man could venture no conclusion, that he was blind to God and himself and the world in which he lived, and that the more he groped the farther he strayed. Doubt gave rise to the celebrated prayer, "O God, if there be a God, save my soul, if I have a soul!" It was hard to believe in anything; hard, and easy. For while some doubted, others ran after every new revelation, seeking after signs, believing in miracle workers, clairvoyants, winking pictures—anything provided it was incredible or expensive. In the twin moods of doubt and credulity men looked for something other than what had satisfied their fathers.

With this unrest went a longing for confession, so that Robertson heard many an account of wandering faith. The people could trust him. He half-revealed himself to them. In his sermons he probed his own experience. What he discovered in those solitary depths he took to God in confession and prayer. Then he had the grit to trace for others the path of spiritual pilgrimage. He found hope in the Bible. In his Brighton ministry he dealt with Abraham, Jacob, Moses,

David, Elijah, John the Baptist, Thomas—each in his time a pilgrim of the lonesome road, each with his special burden of doubt. Were the people of the nineteenth century the first to ask questions? Was Brighton the first city to backslide from God? Were the members of Trinity Chapel the first to begin a quest of faith? There before Robertson was the congregation with all its needs. From the mass a single face, and another and then another, took sharp focus. One by one they had sought him out, expecting sympathy and receiving it. Other hearts opened to him because he spoke truly of his own.

Not every visitor who came to Robertson was on the verge of confession. The pastor enjoyed good conversation for its own sake. Once started, he was a lively talker, and when he met a person who had something to talk about, the conversation took wings. He was introduced to a captain who had just returned from the Cape. Robertson listened to adventures of Kaffirland warfare, in which his two brothers, Charles and Harry, were to receive honorable mention. "The risk and excitement," he said, "are more real than the being badgered by old ladies of both sexes in a place like Brighton." He could almost see the Kaffirs' slim black bodies slipping through the grass like snakes; the ambush; the goading and burning of English prisoners; the chieftain drinking from the hollow of a human skull. Many of the British soldiers were equally savage. Drunken, brutalized by war, they had no mercy for their victims. As if in reproach for self-pity, Robertson exclaimed: "This is man! and these things are going on while we sit by our fireside and complain of *ennui*, or weariness, or religious persecution or scandal, or some other trifling gnat-bite."

About the same time he saw a friend with the blunt nose

and outthrust jaw of a boxer—cheerful, bustling, tough-fibered Henry Crabb Robinson—"Old Crabb," lawyer, news correspondent, citizen of the world, and intimate friend of the famous. For a period of fifty years this man was proud to have known almost every celebrated author in England and Germany. He had studied at Jena in the "great time" of Wieland, Schiller, and Goethe. Robinson had taught Madame De Staël. He had been the traveling companion of Wordsworth, the friend of Coleridge and Southey, Lamb and Rogers, and their different groups. In the young minister he found a good conversationalist and congenial friend.

Crabb Robinson was not a brilliant thinker. But he had wide interests, the gift of enthusiasm, and a scribbling vigilance that gave full record of all that he saw and felt. He liked Robertson, and in more than one drawing room came to his defense. One evening the two friends, old and young, had tea together in Brighton. A famous talker, Robinson was "full of anecdote, and more than I ever saw him anxious for religious information. Last Sunday's sermon seems to have struck him, and appeared very original." The old man mentioned a party that he had attended, where the incumbent of Trinity Chapel was the object of criticism, accusations of heterodoxy, and the like. Crabb Robinson had only one thing to tell the critics about Robertson: "I never heard him without having some stumbling-block removed; and doctrines that appeared to me absurd in the orthodox system shown to be in harmony with eternal reason and truth."

Robertson attracted the young as well as the old. One person, younger than he, remembered his gracious manner: "The testimony of his oldest friends is true—he listened to the crude theories and dogmatic opinions of a young man with a sympathy which awoke thought, and a compassion

which did not offend." For three weeks this person was stay-
ing in the same house with Robertson. After dinner they
walked until about ten o'clock, and a little later met with
others for historical games, writing poetry, and "capping"
verses. "The humour with which he put down ignorance, the
playfulness with which he exposed a mistake by wilfully
making another of the same kind twice as bad, the frown with
which he pounced upon an offender whose metre was halting,
the bright smile with which he welcomed a new thought or
happy expression, the social art with which he brought into
relief and elucidated our different characters"—these made
the hours fly, and left a pleasant memory with those who
knew him in his lighter moments. The friend used four nouns
to describe Robertson—lightness, freshness, eagerness, and
energy—but he did not guess at the truer word, loneliness.

While his younger acquaintances rode, Robertson sometimes walked beside them, keeping up with the pace of the
horses. "It was wonderful how much he made us see." He
noticed the sunlight slanting through the trees overhead. He
pointed to the orange fungus making a bright splotch of
color beside the path. He was on the lookout for animal
furrows and the nests of birds. "I shall not easily forget his
delight when the woodcocks came and he was the first to see
one, nor the way in which he absolutely ran over with stories
of their manner of life. He seemed to me to know all the
poetry which referred to animals, and quoted Wordsworth
till I wondered at his memory."

Another friend, Julian Charles Young, was an Anglican
minister. Periodically, on business or pleasure, Mr. Young
went to Brighton. He would stop to see Robertson, and often
would walk with him on the downs. Starting out on a rural
walk, they took back streets so as to escape the crowds on

the eastern or western cliffs. When they crossed a busy thoroughfare, Young said, hats were doffed right and left. As long as they were in Brighton, Robertson was constrained and reticent. But once on the downs, he seemed to expand. His conversation was familiar, often confidential, always lofty and never flippant. Somehow he was more himself when others were not looking on.

At times when Robertson was lonesome or overwrought, he set out for the downs with no human companion. Walking there brought a truce between his restless body and his weary mind. Away from the turmoil of Brighton, calm ensued, and he listened to the voice of God in the hush of exhausted excitement. Earth seemed lifted nearer heaven on the downs, which stood open to the sky, broad and green, and swelling fold on fold. He looked across the gentle interchange of hill and valley, to other slopes beyond and far away, melting in the haze to softer hue. The peace of the hills rested upon him. The bleating of the distant flock, the faint bark of the shepherd's dog, and the lowing of cattle in some faroff hollow gently stirred the air. Coarse lowland sounds did not penetrate the silence of the hills, yet there was a mysterious harmony, subdued, always at a distance, as if the music of the spheres had filtered down to earth in the oversong of birds in flight. There was something of more than earth on the downs, something of heaven and of God.

Much as he loved the downs, when Robertson came back to Brighton his loneliness returned. He had to keep in touch with other people. When he could not talk to them, he wrote. His correspondence was prodigious. Once he said, "I begin to reply briefly to your letter." When he finished, the answer had stretched to more than fifteen hundred words! In the year 1849 he began writing to several friends who cherished his letters. His messages showed the fixed points in his thought, his moods, and the vagrant turnings of his mind. He was no mere ecclesiastical gossip. He wrote about everybody and everything, on subjects literary, social, political, and scientific, as well as religious. His thought ranged from the catechism to Fichte and Lessing, from Robespierre to Baron Munchausen's horse, from the laws of chemistry to the writings of Tennyson and Keble. Through it all, usually in undertone, but swelling now and then into fuller volume, ran the strain of solitariness.

From day to day in the autumn of 1849, he read from John Keble's poems in *The Christian Year*. In his letters Robertson often made some comment, appreciative or explanatory, on these lines of sacred verse. One November evening he came to the beautiful hymn on the loneliness of the soul:

> Why should we faint and fear to live alone,
>   Since all alone, so Heaven has will'd, we die,
> Nor even the tenderest heart, and next our own,
>   Knows half the reasons why we smile and sigh?

That same evening—it was Sunday—he took up his pen: "I am very unfit to write; much tired, dispirited, and lonely." Several factors may have combined to bring about his mood. Autumn winds had brought rain from the sea. The earth was like a sponge. Sunday was dark, cheerless; fog spread from horizon to horizon without a patch of light. Buildings loomed dim through the mist. It would have been difficult for anyone to be lighthearted in such weather. What was worse, Robertson said, "I spoke very badly indeed, though fluently, and this has added an oppressing sensation of impotency to sadness. I know that it is partly physical; that I am not myself, nor master of my fancies, and, therefore, I will not let my pen pour out feelings of which I might be ashamed, and which certainly I should disown to-morrow. . . . You can have little idea of the gloomy thoughts with which I have to struggle on many Sunday evenings."

These letters reveal what the sermons of Robertson strongly suggest: the physical anguish that went with his loneliness. An organic disease had begun to claw at his brain. He confessed that he was sometimes tortured "to a state in which I could call Dante's conceptions of the 'Inferno' dull. For example, the thought of drudging on here at the same work, unvaried; two sermons a Sunday, inspiration by clockwork for several years, is simply the conception of an impossibility. I want perpetually the enthusiasm which comes from fresh views of duty and untrodden paths of usefulness—new impulses from the heart; yet that in itself, when it comes, leaves me worn to the extremity of endurance."

Then came the still, small voice, with the feeling of a Presence that made loneliness vanish from his thought. "I do not know that I have felt so softened and humbled for a long time as at the hour of prayer this morning; more gentleness seemed to distill upon my soul than I have felt for a long time. I could have wept, not happy nor sanguine, but subdued and humanised tears. I do not know exactly why; at least, it would take long to explain the train of thought. But it ran very little upon myself, or upon my own concerns. Wordsworth, in his account of the revulsion by which young disappointment passes into something resigned, and almost cheerful at last, speaks of a kind of sweet melancholy and repose found—

> In the soothing thoughts which spring
> Out of human suffering."

IX

The Groundwork of the Sermon

TEACHING the Bible was the core of Robertson's entire ministry. In the spirit of the collect, he read, marked, learned, and inwardly digested the Holy Scriptures. "This Word of God has held a thousand nations for thrice a thousand years spellbound; held them by an abiding power, even the universality of its truth; and we feel it to be no more a collection of books, but *the* Book." No small part of his power lay in the source of his preaching. He loved to realize the past, to bring it before his eyes, and to make it as distinct and real as if he had lived in it; to know David or Paul as a friend; to identify himself with the man of the Bible, thought with thought, sense with sense, until he knew the inner windings of his character. Robertson's teaching was saturated with the Bible.

For his Sunday morning sermon he often chose a text about a Bible character in action, preferring to deal with a man who lived the truth, rather than with some abstraction. For the expository lecture in the afternoon he selected a longer passage of Scripture. "The difference between the two," he explained, "was that in the morning we took for our subject a single text, and endeavoured to exhaust that;

but in the afternoon a chapter, and endeavoured to expound
the general truth contained therein. The sermon was horta-
tory and practical; the lecture was didactic. The first appealed to the heart and conscience; the second rather to the
analytic faculty."

Exposition was a good teaching method. It was not the
most popular sermon form by any means, but for the afternoon discourse he chose solidity over against outward at-
tractiveness. Robertson's thought had time to ripen, for he
had a plan. In six years of expository lectures he covered
First and Second Samuel, Acts, Genesis, and Corinthians—
that, and nothing more! He worked through a book, chapter
by chapter, week by week. Thus he gave the full symmetry
of each author's purpose, instead of snipping off an occasional twig of doctrine. Several passages forced themselves
upon him that he would otherwise have overlooked or evaded;
but he felt that to be honest he must not pass by anything
merely because it was difficult. He read his Bible, knew much
of it by heart, and interpreted Scripture in its fullness.

"Now in explaining any passage of Scripture, two things
have to be done: first, to put ourselves in possession of the
circumstances under which the words were spoken, to endeavour to realise the society, persons, feelings, and customs
of the body of men, and of the time, to whom and in which
the passage was addressed; secondly, to discern in what
point and principles the passage corresponds to our circumstances. For otherwise we misinterpret Scripture, misled by
words and superficial resemblances. This is what Christ
meant in His description of the wise Scribe, who 'brings out
of his treasure things new and old.' For the great office of
the expounder is to adapt old principles to new circumstances, and to read the present through the past."

In the study he formed the ideals for his sermons. One of the rules was to preach positively, not negatively. Robertson uttered his convictions rather than his doubts. He said that truth wins, not in debate, but in demonstrating the spirit of truthfulness. "It is an endless work to be uprooting weeds: plant the ground with wholesome vegetation, and then the juices which would have otherwise fed rankness will pour themselves into a more vigorous growth; the dwindled weeds will be easily raked out then. It is an endless task to be refuting error. Plant truth, and the error will pine away." In a conversation with Dr. King, his physician, Robertson admitted surprise that his sermons had been largely unmolested, despite grumblings about the preacher.

Dr. King answered: "I can tell you the reason. You preach positively instead of negatively, you state truths which they cannot deny: they only can talk of tendencies, consequences, etc.; they can only say it is dangerous, they dare not say it is false; if you were once to preach defensively or controversially, it would be all over with you, and it would do your heart and mind harm besides; but every one sees that you have a message and a truth to establish; you set up your truth, and they are dismayed to find, if *that* be true, their view is knocked down, but you did not knock it down."

Another rule was to preach suggestively, not exhaustively or dogmatically. By this he meant that he tried to make one large truth clear and luminous. The mass of hearers did not want or need the cold necessities of logic. They wished to understand the practical message of Christianity, not for Sunday alone, but for every day, and not in the church alone, but in the home and shop as well. Robertson was not a bond-slave to the jargon of any religious party; nor did he con-

sider his judgment infallible. Yet some who heard him acted
as if they had circumscribed all truth; they came to church
to hear him repeat the proper words in a sermon, or to mark
his straying from the beaten track. To Robertson, truth took
form in life rather than in words. By "true" doctrine he
meant an experience that each man or woman could verify
in daily life. He preached doctrine—sacrifice, atonement, reconciliation, salvation—always in terms of God's dealing with
the individual human soul. In short, he made religion practical, put doctrine to work, and assumed that the man in the
pew brought his brains as well as his heart to the House of
God.

He also believed that Christian faith works from the inward to the outward, not vice versa. This was his own
method: he felt; he thought; he spoke; he acted. Robertson
kept saying that righteousness "is from within: it is life: it
is God in the soul of man: it is the life of the spirit. It is not
a creed got by heart: it is not a set of habits acquired: it is
not a circle of customs scrupulously observed." Why did
politicians attempt to work from the outward to the inward,
as when Britain tried to force episcopacy on Scotland and
Protestantism on Ireland? Why did reformers twist things
about, trying to remove all hazards and putting temptations
out of sight, instead of toughening the man within to resist
and overcome his lot? Reform? By all means! But faith
starts to work inwardly, and forces its way outward into the
world.

In choosing his text and in outlining the message, Robertson laid stress on the principle of balance. Partly for this
reason he excelled in writing a sermon with only two main
parts. One of the balanced texts on which he preached was,
"Ye shall know the truth, and the truth shall make you free."

The topic was "Freedom by the Truth." "The Principle of the Spiritual Harvest" grew out of the words of Paul, "Be not deceived; God is not mocked: for whatsoever a man soweth, that shall he also reap. For he that soweth to his flesh shall of the flesh reap corruption; but he that soweth to the Spirit shall of the Spirit reap life everlasting." "Christ's Estimate of Sin" had as its origin, "The Son of man is come to seek and to save that which was lost." The sermon on "Prayer" dealt with the surrender of Christ: "O my Father, if it be possible, let this cup pass from me: nevertheless, not as I will, but as Thou wilt." Each of these texts embraces the human element and the divine, and each has in it either balanced or contrasting thoughts.

Usually Robertson, in arranging his ideas for preaching, set the object before the means to its attainment, the theory before the practice, the fact before the meaning, the general before the specific, the true before the false, the good before the evil. With religious controversy raging all around him, he taught that "truth is made up of two opposite propositions." His thought was dialectic. He did not go in search of a *via media*, "in some middle, moderate, timid doctrine which skillfully avoids extremes," but rather he looked for a doctrine large enough to include apparently hostile thoughts. Forms of statement that seemed to clash, concerning baptism, for example, he insisted were often two ways of looking at a single fact. In his teaching ministry he made an honest effort to reconcile not only man with man, but truth with truth.

This was the tested formula of Robertson. He took one clear thought and let it dominate the sermon; he developed it positively, not negatively; suggestively, not dogmatically; from the inward to the outward; and with frequent use of balance and contrast. He found points of agreement in conflicting dogmas, and since he was convinced that God has power to transform lives, he looked for "the soul of goodness in things evil."

The sermons were impressive in scope, but did not scatter thought; they grappled with large subjects, but were almost always accurate in detail. Robertson's words revealed his passion for truth, his sympathy with human weakness that longs for divine power, and his stand against social wrongs. The sermons embodied practical thinking and sane advice, and showed indirectly the minister's knowledge of nature and the arts. Robertson did not pad. His singleness of aim in toiling for clear expression brought about sermons that were artful but never mannered. He handled big themes, such as Providence, Election, Sanctification, and the Church. Two theological questions in particular exercised his mind: first, the way of arriving at certainty in matters of religion; and second, the true idea of redemption and expiation. His central doctrine was the person of Christ, and because of its massiveness, his other thoughts gravitated toward this center.

To preach Christ, he said, is to preach the doctrines of Christ, that men may be saved. The Gospel is not a bribe to enter heaven, or a threat of hell; it is the life, death, and Resurrection of Christ "being made manifest in our body." On the whole Robertson's aim as a preacher was not to effect violent conversions, but to give his people a growing consciousness of the breadth, length, depth, and height of God's love in Christ. Robertson's task was ministerial; Christ's alone was priestly. "Therefore the whole work of the Christian ministry consists in declaring God as reconciled to man; and in beseeching with every variety of illustration, and every degree of earnestness, men to be reconciled to God."

One secret of his power in Brighton was the fact that Robertson preached doctrine; but he always preached it for the sake of life. His most doctrinal sermons were more or less ethical, just as the words of Christ weave truth and duty into a whole fabric.

Robertson was thoroughly at home in teaching Biblical ethics; that is, the bearing of the Scriptures on practical everyday problems. He thought that Christianity had been presented "too much as theology, too little as the religion of daily life; too much as a religion of feeling, too little as a revelation of principles: too much as a religion only for the individual, and too little as a religion for the nation and the world." The bulk of his ethical preaching came in the afternoon lectures, but on Sunday mornings, too, he instructed Christian men in the fine art of living together. Robertson preached on such topics as "The Message of the Church to Men of Wealth" and "Christ's Judgment Respecting Inheritance." He dealt with the "natural affinities" of family life. He spoke about "The Tongue," "Purity," and "Worldliness."

Teaching Christian ethics also included many sermons on the social order. Robertson preached to raise funds for the Humane Society, whose object was to rescue persons from drowning, sunstroke, freezing, suffocation, or the like. "The Orphanage of Moses" was on behalf of the Brighton home for parentless girls. Robertson also gave a number of election sermons. In one of these he said, "I have endeavoured to keep entirely unseen my own political views. I may have failed, but not voluntarily." He upheld principles, not parties, and declared that it was "better to be a true man on the side of wrong than a false man on the side of right." On whatever topic he spoke, Robertson was guided by the truth that this is God's world, and that man is God's instrument. His entire message, and especially his ethical teaching, sprang from "a sense of mercy and a sense of hope."

Even with so complete a theory of his work—Biblically, doctrinally, and ethically—a minister may go stale. But the sermons of Robertson went "from strength to strength." The reason was that into each new effort he put the stock and surplus of long, hard study. He was an intense reader. A bookman, in whose shop the minister liked to browse, visited Robertson's home; he afterward recalled that the library was not large, but it impressed him as having been chosen with extreme care. To the bookseller, Robertson was less a general than a special reader. He did not scatter his efforts; he dug hard along certain lines; he read deeply rather than widely.

Thus he worked—slowly, methodically, with pains to get to the heart of what he read. He advised one of his correspondents to go through Ruskin slowly, and to finish no more than a few pages at a time. Study. Think over each chapter. Write the headings on a slip of paper. Each day run over the principles of the day before. Ask if the author is right or wrong. This was not the way to read many books, he said, but it was the way to read much. Still he was amazed at all that would evade his memory, as if reading were no more than the mechanical act of turning pages. He was frank to admit that a hundred books had evaporated from his conscious mind; he might as well never have seen them. Therefore, he took his own advice. He tested himself. He wrote down an abstract of a book, not in the author's words but in his own, giving the principal thoughts. This habit enabled him to grasp what he read, and fixed the theme in his memory for years.

Naturally there were some books through which he hurried; a work on travel by Miss Martineau did not consume many hours. "I began that book at sunrise, and finished it a little after breakfast-time. It gave me a healthy glow of feeling, a more cheerful view of life." For the most part, however, he went slowly. He seldom skimmed; he read hard or not at all. Once he mentioned studying *Macbeth* far into the night. The murder scene was so vivid that he felt a creeping hesitation as he climbed the stairs—"and in very shame [I] was obliged to walk down again through the dark passages, to convince myself that I was not a child haunted with unreal terrors."

By sunlight and lamplight the reading went on, as if the outcome of a war depended on it. Large areas of knowledge were opening to him as an Englishman, as vast and unexplored as the political empire. Indeed, the two went together. New language studies, comparative mythology, folklore, and a hundred other subjects were being added to the outer range of the humanities. Robertson did not have time to master all of these specialties; but his interests were far-flung. In preparation for the expository lectures he mastered everything that he could find on his period, whether in history, ethnology, or archaeology of the Bible. At the same time he read devotional works, poetry, and books in many outlying areas of knowledge. Yet in one of his loneliest hours he wrote: "I read Shakespeare, Wordsworth, Tennyson, Coleridge, Philip Van Artevelde, for views of man to meditate upon, instead of theological caricatures of humanity; and I go into the country to *feel* God; dabble in chemistry, to feel awe of Him; read the life of Christ, to understand, love, and adore Him; and my experience is closing into this, that I turn with disgust from everything to Christ."

On coming to Brighton, he had determined to "study

scripture-books thoroughly through, histories separately
and thoroughly." He also looked for stability in regular
tasks; he wished to avoid desultory visits and fitful reading.
Interruptions broke in on his best-laid plans. His sermons
were not academic or prepared with the quiet leisure of
scholarship; they were the product of a busy pastor's life.
To save time he jotted down what he must do each day, fixing
his hours. He did not have to ask himself continually, "What
next?" If he did not do all that was on the schedule, he ac-
complished more than he omitted. At times he slackened pace,
or lost interest, or was cut short by a visitor, yet he had the
knack of getting things done. He forced himself to the
"precious bane" of routine. He said that he had to work "up
to the collar, hot and hard, without intermission to the last,
not leaving time or coolness to feel the parts that were galled,
and raw, and wrung."

Still he had time for little Charlie. In outlining his day
Robertson made room for teaching his son geography from
ten to eleven in the morning. The hours before that he spent
in his own studies. In 1850 he combed works chiefly bearing
on Genesis, along with such books as Pritchard's *Physical
History of Man*, Wilkinson's *Egyptians*, and "two of the
best Germans, who in all matters of research are immeasur-
ably before the English: exhausting a subject." After the
geography lesson, Robertson went back to his books until
about one o'clock. Following luncheon he talked with visitors
or wrote to his friends. He hurried to the post at fifteen minutes to three. Several days in the week he taught at the local
training school, lecturing on Daniel and St. John. "Then
visits to the sick, engagements, walk, etc. Dinner at six, listening to Charlie's prattle till eight, then study again till
ten." He admitted that he kept these hours only in "an

approximating way," but as a preacher he gave himself wholeheartedly to the Gospel of Work.

Sometimes his thought was slow in gathering momentum. On Monday it seemed utterly hopeless that he could eke out two more sermons before Saturday night. His mind was numb. In such hours he made ready for the pulpit by reading an inspiring book—even if it did not bear directly on his topic—until his blood ran fast, and his thoughts began to stir, gather, precipitate, and take on new color and substance. "I know something myself of hard work; I know what it is to have had to toil when the brain was throbbing, the mind incapable of originating a thought, and the body worn and sore with exhaustion; and I know what it is in such an hour, instead of having recourse to those gross stimulants to which all worn men, both of the higher and lower classes, are tempted, to take down my Sophocles or my Plato (for Plato was a poet), my Goethe or my Dante, Shakespeare, Shelley, Wordsworth or Tennyson; and I know what it is to feel the jar of nerve gradually cease, and the darkness in which all life had robed itself to the imagination become light, discord pass into harmony, and physical exhaustion rise by degrees into a consciousness of power."

Although he planned well ahead, the sermon outline sometimes came to him with the surprise that an unforeseen idea brings even to the man of talent. Vision and thought and words strangely and suddenly fused together; then he began to write, as if he had gigantic energy, as if there were too many thoughts to crowd on the paper all at once. "It is a grand thing," he said, "when in the stillness of the soul, thought bursts into flame, and the intuitive vision comes like an inspiration . . . winged as it were with lightning." He first made full notes; then he drew up an outline; afterward he put down his thoughts freely, often twice or three times over, into a connected theme; finally, he made a skeleton, which he sometimes carried into the pulpit, and almost never used.

Experience taught him that memory is of no avail without some organizing principle. A teacher must know where he is going. "All public speakers know the value of method. Persons not accustomed to it imagine that a speech is learnt by heart. Knowing a little about the matter, I will venture to say that if any one attempted that plan, either he must have a marvellous memory, or else he would break down three times out of five. It simply depends upon correct arrangement. The words and sentences are left to the moment; the thoughts methodised beforehand; and the words, if the thoughts are rightly arranged, will place themselves. But upon the truthfulness of the arrangement all depends."

An outline by Robertson was vertebrate. "Christian Progress by Oblivion of the Past," delivered August 12, 1849, had Robertsonian structure. The basic idea was that of Philippians 3:13, 14—"Brethren, I count not myself to have apprehended: but this one thing I do, forgetting those things which are behind, and reaching forth unto those things which are before, I press toward the mark for the prize of the high calling of God in Christ Jesus." He addressed men and women who were already Christians, and treated the doctrine of sanctification. His thought was rugged and original, at the same time showing none of the bizarre effects of one who strains after novelty. The form adapted itself to the thought; there was no pumping in or slopping over.

In his usual manner Robertson had two main points. This

was not a juggler's balancing act, but a habit of mind, through training almost an instinct. The body of the sermon contained these thoughts:

I. *The apostle's object—progress*
   A. Perfection is his unreached mark.
      1. The Christian aims at no less.
      2. But perfection is unattainable in this life.
   B. To this object the apostle gives himself with singleness of aim.
      1. Perfection is being, not doing.
      2. Progress is *becoming* Christ-like.
   C. The apostle attains the prize.
      1. He aims at the "mark," not the prize.
      2. Spurious goodness seeks only reward.
      3. The prize is beyond this life.
II. *The apostle's means—oblivion of the past.*
   A. It is wise to forget the days of childish innocence.
      1. Early innocence is only ignorance of evil.
      2. Innocence is gone—forget it.
   B. It is wise to forget the days of youth.
      1. In later years the tendency is to look back.
      2. One should live in the present.
      3. One should keep pressing forward.
   C. It is wise to forget past errors.
      1. A self-accusing temper hinders progress.
      2. The Christian makes the best of what he is.
      3. The Gospel brings the inspiring news of pardon.

One of Robertson's strongest messages, however, had three points. The sermon dealt with "The Three Crosses on Calvary." Instead of putting the Cross of Christ last, as many preachers would do, Robertson placed it first. In other words, the central Cross dominated the entire scene. Then came the stark antithesis of the thief on the left hand: "As he lived, so he died." Finally, there was the sinner on the right hand who confessed, "We receive the due rewards of our deeds: but this man hath done nothing amiss." Thus Robertson preached on:

   I. The Dying Hour of Devotedness
  II. The Dying Hour of Impenitence
III. The Dying Hour of Penitence

What could be more simple, more dramatic, more logical, or more profound?

Using his utmost skill, Robertson shaped his sermon ideas into a connected whole. The impulse came from believing that he should interpret God's truth in the Bible for the needs of his time. As doctrine, the sermons were positive, fresh, and thought-stirring. As exposition, they showed breadth of view and independence of mind. As appeals to the heart and conscience, they possessed the eloquence of deep personal faith. All this is evident from his published works. But the reader cannot see the turn of Robertson's head or the look in his eye; cannot hear that deep voice pause, trembling at the awfulness of the words; cannot sense the full sway of the personality in his teaching:

"Learn this: When we live the Gospel so, and preach the Gospel so, sinners will be brought to God. We know not yet the Gospel power; for who trusts, as Jesus did, all to that? Who ventures, as He did, upon the power of Love, in sanguine hopefulness of the most irreclaimable? who makes *that*, the divine humility of Christ, 'the Gospel'? More than by eloquence, more than by accurate doctrine, more than by ecclesiastical order, more than by any doctrine trusted to by the most earnest and holy men, shall we and others, sinful rebels, outcasts, be won to Christ by that central truth of all the Gospels—the entireness of the Redeemer's sympathy. In other words, the Love of Jesus."

X

The Art of Preaching

ROBERTSON cast his sermons in a rare alloy of dialectic strength and imaginative charm. Because he was a hard worker in the study, thoroughly preparing in thought and word for a pulpit, he was a mighty preacher. Yet study and method were not sufficient to explain how he transformed long habits of thought and life. He had something beyond the outline or the words. Intensity was the secret of his power. Lady Byron said of Robertson, "His very calm is a hurricane." She did not mean in loudness, but in driving force. The truth that he taught was a living thing, which called for the daring and loyalty of a soldier. Anyone who heard him knew that here was a man bringing out his inmost thoughts; and though his critics balked at one sermon or another, there was no denying that he spoke with the energy of conviction. He entered the pulpit in the full vigor of manhood. Yet each Sunday exhausted something of his vital power. He was burning up his strength; every sermon was an unreturning flame. He kept on giving all that he had to give.

"I feel the wear and tear of heart and mind in having so constantly, and in so unassisted a way, to speak on solemn subjects." None the less he spoke. In 1849 he came into the full powers of his calling. The name of Robertson was a byword now in Brighton, and Trinity Chapel, already full, reached the overflow. He stood in the pulpit as if he pleaded with men. His blue eyes, deep-set, had an earnest look; a friend said that they "left their light with you when he had gone." His posture was erect, and he spoke with few gestures and little movement; only an occasional uplifting of the hand, or an ever-so-slight stamp of the foot. The most impressive thing about him was his voice, low and musical, full of restrained feeling, in its varied tones and cadences like the voice of the sea.

Those who often heard him could never forget Robertson's voice; something in it plucked strangely at the heartstrings. One who had frequently worshiped at Trinity Chapel recalled the accents of that deep voice: "I have never heard the liturgy read as Mr. Robertson read it. He carried its own spirit with him; and those prayers, so often degraded by careless reading into mere forms, were from his voice felt to be instinct with a Divine light and spirit. The grave earnestness and well-weighed emphasis with which he read the Gospel of the day, were absolutely an exposition of its meaning." The voice of Robertson gave life to the forms of worship, and stirred the congregation when he began to preach. He announced the text. He spoke quietly but feelingly, then gathered volume as thought warmed and flowed into utterance. The worshiper who spoke of his reading the liturgy said also of his preaching:

"I cannot describe to you in words the strange sensation during his sermon, of union with him and communion with one another which filled us as he spoke. . . . Nor can I describe to you the sense we had of a higher Presence with us as he spoke—the sacred awe which filled our hearts—the hushed stillness in which the smallest sound was startling—the calmed eagerness of men who listened as if waiting for a word of revelation to resolve the doubt or to heal the sorrow of a life—the unexpected light which came upon the faces of some when an expression struck home and made them feel —in a moment of high relief from pain or doubt—this man speaks to *me*, and his words are inspired by God. And when the close came, and silence almost awful fell upon the church, even after a sigh of relief from strained attention had ceased to come from all the congregation, I have often seen men so rapt that they could not move till the sound of the organ aroused them to the certainty that the preacher had ceased to speak."

It was as if minister and congregation met halfway. Robertson often used the style of direct address. He was not afraid of personal pronouns. In one passage of one hundred and fourteen words, he said "you" ten times. In the sermon on "Christian Progress by Oblivion of the Past," the speaker put himself in the place of the hearer. "It is natural to say, 'All that was well enough for one so transcendentally gifted as Paul to hope for: but I am no gifted man; I have no iron strength of mind; I have no sanguine hopefulness of character; I am disposed to look on the dark side of things; I am undetermined, weak, vacillating; and then I have a whole army of passions and follies to contend with . . .' First let a man know that all his past is wrong and sinful; then let him fix his eye on the love of God in Christ loving him—even him, the guilty one. Is there no strength in that—no power in the knowledge that all that is gone by *is gone*, and that a fresh, clear future is open?"

Most of what he said was in personal terms that anyone could understand. A sprinkling of words may have been obscure; a shop boy would hardly know the precise meaning of "transcendentally gifted" or "sanguine hopefulness." The minister sometimes let philosophy get the upper hand; for instance, "Omnipresence in space is equivalent to ubiquity in time." Again, speaking to the yokels in the nearby village of Hurstpierspont, he aimed too high. But the fact is that shop boys, rustics, artisans, and others who labored with their hands, admired the preaching of Robertson. When they could not understand his words, still they trusted the man. Robertson believed in the simplicity of the Gospel, as well as the simplicity of sermons, but by simplicity he did not mean shallowness. The "simple Gospel" is unmixed, unadulterated. "There must be an earnestness, candour, patience, and a certain degree of intelligence as well as a sort of sympathy between the minds of the preacher and his hearers, and there must be a determination to believe that no man who endeavours to preach the Gospel will deliberately and expressly say what he knows to be false or wrong."

Along with this direct style went a feeling for beauty. Robertson clothed his thought with images. In the preceding century ministers had thought of the sermon as a logical demonstration or some historical evidence of faith. They believed that religious emotion was unorthodox; hence they admired the typical and abstract; they created systems and beheld "the spacious firmament" revolving under general laws. These ministers passed by individual experience. They largely ignored touch, sight, smell, taste, and sound. In bewigged dignity they analyzed, generalized, moralized, and latinized. Early in the nineteenth century, however, writers of every sort rediscovered persons and things. Robertson, among them, used concrete words of sense and feeling. Like Amos and Bunyan, he used similitudes.

Glints of color and flashes of motion made his sentences into pictures. Robertson selected familiar events and common objects, such as the sunflower, the butterfly, the swallow's flight, insects in amber, stones along the beach, a flag, a sundial, a telescope, a magnet, the railroad chuffing into the station on Saturday night, the vessel borne headlong on the breakers and splintered on the sands near Brighton. Once in a while he used a longer illustration; but more often the sharp outlines of nature, in a quick, vivid word-picture, served his realistic purpose.

He borrowed illustrations from life more than from books. He showed a person in an ordinary situation: the student with his volumes, the workman with a hod of bricks, the chemist with his retorts, each finding or shunning a Christian truth. In his preaching Robertson gathered examples from all levels of life. He had learned to call nothing common or unclean. The beggar, gambler, merchant, statesman, criminal, Hottentot, minister, soldier and sailor, harlot, miner, artist, landlord and tenant, and a whole legion of those who did the world's work and fought its wars, passed before his inner eye.

Robertson was a keen critic of daily life. "Go to the intemperate man in the morning, when his head aches, his hand trembles, his throat burns, and his whole frame is relaxed and unstrung: he is ashamed, he hates his sin, and would not do it. Go to him at night, when the power of habit is on him like a spell, and he obeys the mastery of his craving. He can use the language of Romans 7:—'That which he would, he does not; but the evil that he hates, that does he.' " One man in moral bondage; that is slavery! The words sound almost like the confession of one in the grip of a loathsome habit. Robertson, in other words, had rare skill in discerning how others felt and acted. There were in his preaching innumerable echoes of his pastoral work. Along with his regular duties ran the counterpoint of martial strains. "No man ever went through a night-watch in the bivouac, when the distant hum of men and the random shot fired told of possible death on the morrow, or watched in a sick-room, when time was measured by the sufferer's breathing or the intolerable ticking of the clock, without a firmer grasp on the realities of life and time."

A beautiful rhythm marked almost everything Robertson said in the pulpit. Sometimes his sentences were short. Again they were ponderous and slow-moving, but they did not rush out in one mighty lung-collapsing blast. When his heart was stirred, Robertson's thoughts flowed from "a well of English undefiled."

"[Christ] not only gave sympathy, but wanted it, too, from others. He who selected the gentle John to be his friend —who found solace in female sympathy, attended by the women who ministered to him out of their substance—who in the trial-hour could bear even to pray without the human presence, which is the pledge and reminder of God's presence —had nothing in Him of the hard, merely self-dependent character. Even this verse testifies to the same fact. A stern spirit never could have said, 'I am not alone; the Father is with Me;' never would have felt the loneliness which needed the balancing truth. These words tell of a struggle—an inward reasoning—a difficulty and a reply—a sense of solitude —'I shall be alone;' and an immediate correction of that, 'not alone—the Father is with me.' "

His words responded to his thoughts like the fall and surge and fall again of ocean waves. His rhythm was the rhythm of speech, infinitely various in pitch and accent, pronunciation, tempo and volume. When Robertson preached there was no iambic singsong. The sermon moved with order and balance, dignity and charm, comprehensiveness and beauty.

Robertson felt what he said, and strove to kindle the feelings of others. All the while he saw the danger of any sermon that led to ungoverned emotion. "Just in proportion as feelings are strong do they require discipline. The temptation is great to indulge from mere pleasure of indulgence, and from the admiration given to feeling. It is easier to gain credit for goodness by a glistening eye, while listening to some story of self-sacrifice, than by patient usefulness. It is easier to get credit for spirituality by thrilling at some impassioned speech on the platform, or sermon from the pulpit, than by living a life of justice, mercy, and truth." If he stirred the feelings with beautiful rhythms, he likewise showed some good cause for action. In his preaching truth was not for the sake of beauty. Beauty served as the garment of living truth.

The peaks of his intensity came when he spoke about the love of God in Christ, but he ventured also into the dark aspects of faith. "We feel that the anger of God is a reality, an awful reality, and that we dare not substitute any other expression." On the human plane, while others talked about mental narrowness, wrong judgment, irresistible passion, and the like, Robertson gave full weight to the fact called sin. Many of his sermons had severe conclusions; even that on "The Sympathy of Christ" ended with the warning: "Win the mind of Christ now—or else His sympathy for human nature will not save you, but only insure the recoil of abhorrence at the last—'Depart from me! I never knew you.'"

Like the Man of Galilee, Robertson spoke at times the language of love in its saddest moods. Yet always with a purpose! Fear has a place in religious experience; its work is not to create holiness but to arrest the conscience. When fear has done its part, then love must perform its higher task. Robertson dealt with judgment on sin; he dealt also with the "absolving power" of the Gospel. He preached for a verdict between the two. Once again he was conscious of a limitation on his preaching. He answered one who had written him a note of thanks:

"I know that spoken words impress, and that impression has its danger as well as its good. Hence I cannot even rejoice without fear, for I confess that at best pulpit instruction seems to me to be as pernicious as it is efficacious. . . . Still, some good is done, but much less than people think; and the drawback, which you correctly state, is one which must always be allowed for as a very large deduction from its apparent effects—I mean the absence of any immediate opportunity of carrying transient impressions into action, and the exhaustion of the feelings which are perpetually stimulated for no definite result. At the highest, all I count on is the probability that in many minds a thought here and there may strike root and grow, mixing with life and ordinary trains of feeling a somewhat higher tone than otherwise might have been, and bringing forth results which will be unconscious and utterly untraceable to the mind that originated them. . . ."

This very limitation added fervor to his preaching. He always had a high purpose, even though he fell short of attaining it. He spoke with utter earnestness because he was treating disorders of the soul. Many of the questions that troubled his friends had been to him matters of personal struggle. There were no pious murmurings about "sweetness and light." Robertson had fought hard for his faith; he knew what it cost; and he was a good counselor for those who still were unsure of themselves. Before the term was invented, he made sermons the vehicle of "pastoral psychiatry." He singled out the individual. He used "life situations." He seemed to say, "Thou art the man!" Then he offered the remedy as he found it in the Gospel, and in human experience —notably his own.

Grappling with a definite problem, Robertson often singled out a Bible character as the focus of his thought. He used the case method in preaching. He sought to show the intricate play of forces within the human heart, to fathom motives, and to set up Christian standards to help the people of Brighton. For example, he dealt with middle-aged religious crisis in the sermon called "Jacob's Wrestling": "The awful feelings about Life and God are not those which characterise our earliest years." Robertson treated doubt in the sermon on Thomas, and dealt with skepticism in the very different but equally telling sermon on Pilate. Joseph learned how to forgive; Balaam perverted his best talents; Zacchaeus overcame a sense of inferiority through "Triumph Over Hindrances." There were several messages about David. One of these in particular, on restoration, had a contemporary ring. The sermon grew out of Psalm 51, which David wrote after committing a double sin. "This Psalm, written three thousand years ago, might have been written yesterday: [it] describes the vicissitudes of spiritual life in an Englishman as truly as of a Jew. 'Not of an age, but for all time.' "

Elijah was the subject of the remarkable sermon on despondency. Why did the prophet give way to discouragement after the victory on Mount Carmel? Why did his most signal failure take place in those points of character where he was strong? Elijah was weary, hungry, travel-worn; he felt that he alone was faithful to God, and that all were against the solitary prophet; he thought that he had no work left to do. On Carmel Elijah seemed to have won his life-aim, yet how suddenly had he become a fugitive! "It was this man—so stern, so iron, so independent, so above all human weakness—of whom it was recorded that in his trial hour he gave way to a fit of petulance and querulous despondency to which there is scarcely found a parallel."

After a diagnosis of Elijah's mood, Robertson went on to describe the cure. "God made him feel the earnestness of life. 'What *doest* thou here, Elijah?' Life is for doing. A prophet's life for nobler doing—and the prophet was not doing, but moaning. . . . Then He went on farther: 'Arise, go on thy way.' That speaks to us: on thy way. Be up and doing; fill up every hour, leaving no crevice or craving of remorse, or a repentance to creep in afterwards. Let not the mind brood on self; save it from speculation, from those stagnant moments in which the awful teachings of the spirit grope into the unfathomable unknown, and the heart torments itself with questions which are insoluble except to an active life. For the awful Future becomes intelligible only in the light of a felt and active Present. Go, return on thy way if thou art desponding—*on thy way;* health of spirit will return."

The words of Robertson did not move like written prose; they were the natural outpouring of extemporaneous speech. Since the mind of the hearer wanders, he knew the value of repetition. In his sermons he expressed one thought in different words, or in the same words, as in the phrase "on thy way." At times he corrected, even contradicted, himself. The sermons lacked Newman's polish, and had none of his irony—oblique, suave, and self-possessed. Robertson was a soul too intent on the message to be concerned with the niceties of rhetoric. In fact, he thought so little of his sermons that he did not keep written copies. Once spoken, as far as he was concerned, the words had fled. He put away scanty records of his enormous work.

Only one sermon by Robertson was published during his lifetime, and that one, strangely, was on the death of Queen Adelaide. He preached a commemoration message in December, 1849. A few weeks later the sermon came out in pamphlet form. Robertson then decided that it would be a long while before he rushed into print again. "I was tormented into publishing, and in an evil hour of weakness gave way, for which weakness I now feel the twinges of remorse." Some of his work had already been pirated. A lecture of the foregoing Advent season unaccountably appeared as "St. Paul's Novitiate." Robertson lamented that the pamphlet was "absurd, curtailed, and in some places absolutely false." He did what little he could to stop such ventures, and in a letter asked his mother to let it be known that all these things were done entirely without his sanction.

His rule was never to retaliate. But he added this statement to the preface of his single published sermon: "The writer takes this opportunity of disowning certain sermons which have been published in his name. They would not have been worth notice, had not the innumerable blunders of thought and expression which they contain been read and accepted by several as his. For this reason he feels it due to himself to state that they are published without his sanction, and against his request, and that he is not responsible for either the language or the ideas." It was bad enough to be criticized for what he said, but far worse to be judged for what he never thought of saying.

Eight volumes of sermons, then, were preserved, almost in

spite of Robertson. At least he had no thought of publication. Sometimes after a service he would write out a digest of his sermon at the request of a friend whom his words had helped; another time he would dictate an after-reminiscence to the younger members of a family in which he was interested; and again, he would dispatch a sermon to one who was sick, or away from Brighton. To the task of preparing and giving the sermon, he added the dead weight of reproducing it. These records, with notes and transcripts kept by different persons in the Chapel, were collected after Robertson's death, compared with his manuscript outlines, and published by his brother. The sermons are not complete; many are fragmentary and roughhewn; and yet they sound the living accents of the preacher.

Some members of the congregation asked if Robertson would allow a shorthand expert to write down his thoughts. In a written answer to their request, the minister gave his fullest and frankest view of preaching:

"Many thanks for your kind note, in which you ask me respecting my feelings on the subject of the shorthand reports of my sermons. I will try to reply in a few words.

"I need scarcely say that it is gratifying—more than gratifying—to know that any of my congregation value my attempts sufficiently to think them worthy of preservation. I am most grateful for it, and for the kindly feeling towards myself of which I am not, perhaps, vain in saying that I accept it as the proof.

"Some time ago you showed me some sermons taken down by a relation of your own, and were kind enough to ask if I disapproved of the continuance of this. Of course, I replied, no. I regretted that any expense should have been incurred, but the thing being private, I could no more object than I could to the practice which many members of the congregation have of taking down the discourses every Sunday, some in ordinary hand, some in shorthand. Mr. —— put the case to me as one in which several kind friends united— and at great expense—to pay a regular reporter, and to preserve the sermons for their common, may I say, edification? and, I understood, my future use, if needed.

"I saw one or two of these, and thought them, from a cursory glance, very accurate. But if you ask me to state candidly what I feel upon the subject, I should say that I think the plan very undesirable. I will not lay much stress on my *great* regret that so large an expense should be incurred for that which is not worth it—for tastes are unaccountable, and fortunes have been given for a tulip-root, streaked in a particular way, or with eight petals instead of seven—I should only say, *I* think you paid dear for your funnily-striped tulip. The Dutchman would say, 'I think not; it is my fancy.'

"But I will only say that there are a great many things said in extempore preaching which pass with the occasion; which are meant so to pass, which have not been deeply examined, and which will, therefore, not bear to be coldly scrutinised in manuscript. A printed or written sermon is always scrutinised as if it claims infallibility, and positive injury might be done to influence if such a hasty expression were stereotyped, as it were. I could not undertake to correct such sermons weekly; I am glad to forget all I say as soon as possible, and, consequently, I should not like to be answerable for such.

"Add to this, that often one at least of the Sunday discourses is insufficiently prepared, the *expressions* utterly unstudied beforehand, the thing itself poor and jejune and worthless. I should not *like* to own it, though, as all but the general *impression* dies with the half-hour of its delivery, it may be well enough as a collection of hints and germs of thought. I think the knowledge, too, that what I said was being taken down in this way would hamper entirely the freeness of expression. As it is, I try to speak unshackled by any attempts to please, to form sentences, and to deprecate disapproval—I do not think I *could* be free were this done. For myself, I would far rather that all should perish except, as I said, the impression the moment after delivery. I preserve few records myself except on a few occasions—I can scarcely bear to read over anything I have said. It would be a relief to me to know that no trace subsisted, except a few hints for my own use, and for future development of the thoughts touched upon.

"I do earnestly trust that this may not seem discourteous. Of course I do not pretend to express strong disapproval if any one should still be determined to proceed. But in reply to your kind question, I have no hesitation in saying that it would give me real pain if the plan were adopted."

Robertson knew his shortcomings, and the limitations of preaching, yet he held back not the slightest ounce of energy in declaring the good news of Christ. One sermon after another was of high order. In December, 1849, Robertson preached fifteen times. On the last day of the year he gave one of his strongest messages, "The Loneliness of Christ." He pictured Jesus alone in the Temple as a boy, alone in trial, alone on the Cross. The Pharisees and Sadducees, the Herodians and people, and finally His disciples had turned from Him and left Him alone; yet not alone, because the Father was with Him. Robertson stressed the grandeur of Christ in loneliness as the strength of every solitary life.

He was preaching to himself, as well as to others who had endured hardness for Christ, not in the heat of battle but in chilly isolation, when called on to fulfill a duty that others looked on coldly, or to stand by a truth that had not yet found welcome in other hearts.

"It is not difficult to get away into retirement, and there live upon your own convictions; nor is it difficult to mix with men, and follow their convictions; but to enter into the world, and there live out firmly and fearlessly according to your conscience, that is Christian greatness." Thus he closed the year. Like his other sermons, the one on loneliness was a spending of himself. "How long will sermonising continue?" he cried out in a letter to a friend. "With all my heart, I hope not to the end of life, unless life is very nearly done." It was Monday, and his letter bore the date of January 1, 1850.

XI

The Strife among Religious Groups

"THERE is something solemn in a commencement, because it reminds us of a close. Twice have I begun, and twice have I finished a book [of Scripture] here. Twice have I reminded you that many present at the beginning of my lectures would never live to hear their termination. Again and again has that prediction been fulfilled. The young, the vigorous, the beautiful have been taken away, and many of us who expected our summons are listening still. But do not forget that there are those among us now who will not hear this course of lectures close." With this sense of urgency Robertson began his lectures on Genesis, which lasted from February, 1850, until May of the following year.

The opening of the new year impressed him once again with the sensation of rushing time, unbroken and irresistible. Robertson wondered how long his ministry would last. His apprehension came out in his letters, and in his sermons. He had reached the age of mid-thirty, when anticipation of the future had lost the brightness of youth, and memory had not yet taken on the patina of age. His plans seemed falling to pieces. Not long before he had thought of writing a work on Inspiration; now he was uninspired. Once he had hoped to become the standard-bearer who would bring the philosophy of Lessing to the English. Poor health forced him to put off that work. In 1850 he felt within himself only the scattered remains of a "once-possible."

Duties thickened upon him. "A year has passed, nearly, since I resolved to live above this world. O God! how little has been done! High, bright, enthusiastic hopes of things impossible, and of things possible still, how they teemed in my imagination. . . . *My* career is done. And yet I do not look on life with any bitter or disappointed feeling, but gently and even gratefully." Time was going; one thing was certain; he ought not to sleep that time away. Robertson trusted in the value and permanence of work, and heeded the imperative call of duty.

Perhaps it is unfortunate that Robertson channeled much of his energy into controversies of the day. Yet these drew from him the vital elements of his character. In 1850 he engaged in three different arguments: one within the Anglican Church on the doctrine of baptism; one against organized skepticism; and one against the Roman Catholics. To the first of these Robertson gave much thought. For some time the Church of England had been troubled by its statement of the doctrine of baptismal regeneration. The controversy reached flood stage early in 1850. The eyes of all England centered on the little hamlet of Brampford Speke-cum-Cowley, where the bishop refused to install a man named Gorham. The reason was that Gorham held Calvinistic views of baptism, and the bishop did not. There followed an ecclesiastical trial that affected every church in the land, including Trinity Chapel. Robertson taught the young men and women who attended confirmation classes:

Q. What is baptism?

A. The authoritative declaration of a fact.

Q. What fact?

A. That I am God's child.

Q. Why then do you say that I am so *made*, in baptism?

A. Being *made*, I mean—*declared to be*.

Q. Explain what you mean.

A. As soon as a king dies, his successor is king. Coronation declares the fact but does not make him king. He was one before, but it corroborates, declares, affirms, seals the fact by a recognized form used for that purpose.

Thus he instructed the young people; and thus he taught the congregation. The more he studied the doctrine, the more his convictions deepened that his own views were faithful to the Prayer Book; so much so that he said: "I would not give up one sentence which it contains upon the subject." In March he preached two sermons on baptism. He contended that the ceremony does not entitle parents to claim saving grace for a child, for a baptized child can still go wrong. Baptism is rather God's sign and seal—made by the Church, administered by the pastor, and agreed to by the parents—that the child belongs to God. Faith, he said, does not create the fact, but only receives it. There were many requests for him to publish his words. He was not quite sure what he ought to do.

"I find the two sermons on baptism have made an impression, in some cases producing great dislike, but in others producing thought, and appearing to shed light on what had before been dark." He had reason to be grateful that his thoughts had helped several members of the congregation. But when these friends asked him to publish his words, he

made up his mind not to do so. Perhaps at some later time
he would recast his sermons so as to have a wider hearing
for his case. For the present, however, he did not concern
himself with the ministry of the written word.

The second controversy came in April, 1850, when Robertson prepared another address for the Working Men's
Institute. This time, however, the members did not invite him
to speak; he asked for the privilege. The organization had
suffered internal strain. The original plan showed signs of
weakness and possible collapse. A movement to bring skeptical works into the library had been gaining ground. Robertson wished to attend one of the meetings "to impart a
healthier tone, if possible," but decided to let the workmen
fight the battle themselves.

Privately and publicly he stood against an interpretation
of life that called "Faith a mistake of the stomach; Love
a titillatory movement occurring in the upper part of the
nape of the neck; Immortality a craving of dyspepsia; God
a fancy produced by a certain pressure upon the grey parts
of the hasty-pudding within the skull." When one of the
foremost members of the Institute died, infidelity was on the
loose. The workmen pestered Robertson to act as leader of
their scattering flock. At last he determined to give the
second address. His position was vulnerable. He had already
taken the abuse of his own order, the clergy, after his first
lecture; and now he strongly opposed some of the men with
whom he had identified himself. He set himself to make "a
desperate attempt" in a public address.

Robertson summoned the working men of Brighton to
meet with him in Town Hall. They came. All the members
of the Institute were there. People of every class gathered
in the large auditorium. The atmosphere was heavy with

suspense. Robertson came forward to speak. Some of the skeptics thought that he stood there as a priest to scold them; they began to groan and hiss; they planned to jibe and hoot him down. But he was British to the backbone. The crowd did not frighten him. Robertson began slowly, softly, with assurance, explaining why he had asked to make an address. His calmness awed the people. The men began an undertone of murmurs. There was a shuffling of feet. More than one workman got up halfway, opened his mouth, then sat down with crimson cheeks as Robertson kept on with his steady flow of words.

When Robertson told why he refused to denounce infidelity, it seemed almost as if the audience stopped breathing. "You have heard of a place called 'Coward's Castle.' Coward's Castle is that pulpit or that platform from which a man, surrounded by his friends, in the absence of his opponents, secure of applause and safe from a reply, denounces those who differ from him. I mean to invite no discussion to-night; and just because there can be no reply, if there were no better reason than that, there shall be no denunciation."

He would not rant against lack of faith. From his years in Brighton he knew that it was a vague and easy charge. He spoke instead on the question of rights. Robertson had heard a great deal about what the working men would like to do, but very little about their "ought." He listened to the catchwords—also vague and easy—on the rights of private judgment, the rights of labor, the rights of man. But when it came to counting heads, only one hundred and thirty-eight men from nearly a thousand actually had voted for skeptical works and inflammatory political tracts in the library. Did these few have reason to force the entrance of books that were disgusting to others and contrary to the stated purpose of the Institute? Robertson thought not. He had heard much on the rights of a minority. The majority also had its rights.

For still another reason he would not unleash his anger on men who doubted. He had known what it was to question everything. In addressing the working men, as at no other time, Robertson described his own struggles. Although he did not parade the doubts as his own, his mind searched back to the fearful days in the Tyrol:

"In the darkest hour through which a human soul can pass, whatever else is doubtful, this at least is certain. If there be no God and no future state, yet, even then, it is better to be generous than selfish, better to be chaste than licentious, better to be true than false, better to be brave than to be a coward. Blessed beyond all earthly blessedness is the man who, in the tempestuous darkness of the soul, has dared to hold fast to these venerable landmarks. Thrice blessed is he, who, when all is drear and cheerless within and without, when his teachers terrify him, and his friends shrink from him, has obstinately clung to moral good. Thrice blessed, because his night shall pass into clear, bright day.

"I appeal to the recollection of any man who has passed through that hour of agony, and stood upon the rock at last, the surges still below him, and the last cloud drifted from the sky above, with a faith, and hope, and trust no longer traditional, but of his own, a trust which neither earth nor hell shall shake thenceforth for ever."

The address proved to be more successful than Robertson had hoped. From that time onward the manhood of Brighton stood behind him. The working men thought over their position. Some wavered; a number split from the Institute and set up a short-lived society; the majority determined to make a fresh start. Robertson counseled quietness. No amount of fanfare and self-puffing would give inward strength. If there were not enough men to join the ranks, then the matter should await a more favorable time. "Better fail silently," he told his friends, "than make another public confession of incapacity." The workmen asked Mr. Robertson to become the president of the new institution. He pledged himself to give an address later on, but the presidency was out of the question. He was glad to help; yet he was unwilling to hold an office that would cast even "the shadow of a shade of suspicion" on the motives of his friendliness to the working men. Thus he wrote in a letter:

"I am *very* anxious that there should be no second failure, but I think that the greatest wisdom and experience are needful to prevent it. . . . The working men have shown that even a right-minded majority is unable to protect itself against a turbulent minority, without the introduction of other elements of society to support them—to support, not dictate; for I should be very sorry to see a majority of gentlemen on the Committee. But they want some, of weight and wisdom, to fall back upon. And indeed, this is the only true democratic principle to my mind—not an oligarchy of the poorest, but a fusion of ranks, with such weight allowed, under checks, as is due to superior means of acquiring information.

"What grieves me to the heart is to see distrust in the minds of working men of those wealthier than themselves; and nothing is more mischievous or unchristian than to gain popularity with them by fostering these feelings, and insinuating that the clergy and the religious and the rich are their enemies, or only espouse their cause for an end.

"I must not accept any high office: I am their friend, but I want nothing from them—not even influence, nor their praise."

Toward the end of the year Robertson engaged in a third controversy. For a number of months after the speech against the skeptics, he addressed the public only as a minister of the Anglican Church. In the autumn he spoke once again as a citizen of Brighton; however, the subject was religious. In 1850 Pope Pius IX parceled England into dioceses, and named Cardinal Wiseman as the head of the new hierarchy. It is likely that the Pope understood neither *Angli* nor *Anglicani*; it is certain that the people of England wanted no popery. From one end of the land to the other there were more than six thousand meetings, goaded by the letter issued from Downing Street by Lord Russell. The Prime Minister complained of many things. He rebuked Anglican pastors who led their flocks step by step to the verge of the Roman precipice. He objected to claims of infallibility, the veneration of saints, the sign of the Cross, the cheeping and muttering of liturgy, the confessional, and the administration of penance and absolution. A hundred thousand noisy anti-popes took up the cry.

Brighton was convulsed. A meeting was called for Thursday, November 14. On the preceding Lord's Day most of the clergy, as if smelling the fires of another Smithfield, raged against the "mother of abominations." Robertson held to a calmer tone. In a sermon on Peter he did not mention the topic that frightened his brethren, until his last words. Speaking of the Pope's action against "free-born Englishmen," he said, "It would have been easy for me to agitate your minds, easy to awake your indignation; for myself I love not such work." He planned to attend the public meeting; but he expected to hear a vast deal of superheated non-sense. He decided to keep his own lips shut.

On Thursday he set out for the Town Hall, and found one of the largest gatherings in the history of Brighton surging into the assembly room. The place was crammed to the window sills. After one or two speeches there were cries for "Robertson." The calls were repeated; finally he rose. Hampered somewhat by lack of preparation, but more by seeing a Roman Catholic acquaintance whom he did not wish to hurt, he gave his views of the papal aggression. "The ground on which I stand here, the reason on which I protest against this Papal Act, is the assumption of infallibility which it contains. It is a claim by an individual man, or by a body of men, of a *right* to press on the consciences of mankind, *authoritatively*, opinions of their own. Whether that view be thundered from the Vatican, or be thundered from Exeter Hall, or come from the assumed infallibility of a private pulpit, be it Dissenting or Church of England, I believe it to be our bounden duty, as Protestants, to protest against it."

Once before, in Cheltenham, Robertson had made a public speech against Romanism. He lectured then on "The Church of England's Independence of the Church of Rome." It was the year of the crash, 1845, when Newman went over to the Roman Church. Robertson's address at that time sounded like a debate, thoroughly historical, dealing in massive detail with Fathers of the Early Church, councils, Bishops Restitorius, Eborius, Adelfius, and the like. As time went on Robertson read less of these recondite matters and thought more of Biblical Christianity. His reasons for opposing the Roman Church became less historical, or rather, more doctrinal. He knew what he thought, and firmly stood his ground. Although he made no apology for plain speaking, he did not defend his claims by a fierce attack on Rome.

In one of the sermons of 1850 he warned his people against "those vituperative and ferocious expressions which are used so commonly against the Church of Rome—unbecoming in conversation, disgraceful on the platform, they are still more unpardonable in the pulpit. I am not advocating that feeble softness of mind which can not speak strongly because it can not feel strongly. I know the value, and in their place, the need of strong words. . . . But now, when Rome is no longer dominant, and the only persecutions that we hear of are the petty persecutions of Protestants among themselves, to use language such as this is not the spirit of a daring reformer, but only the pusillanimous shriek of cruel cowardice which keeps down the enemy whose rising it is afraid of."

Conversion to Rome in the mid-century did not become a fashion or a cultural gesture. On both sides men suffered intensely during the exodus of 1850–51, and the sifting back of later years. Along with other Englishmen, Robertson wrote some ugly things. "Romanism is only an infinitely small and sensualistic embodiment of truths—a living human form shrunk into a mummy." "Purgatory, absolution, Mariolatry, become to me fossils, not lies." "Mountain mass of superstition!" "Poor ignorant Roman Catholics!"

But he showed his more generous nature in writing to one who had left the Church of England. "I wish you had dared to live alone with God for a few years. I believe that you will not find peace long in Rome. But the fact of your being there does not alter my feeling towards you in one iota. Beneath, far beneath all forms of the sight and feeling, I joyfully recognise the unity of that spirit which forms the basis of all true lives. At bottom we mean—all good minds mean—

substantially the same thing; and I look forward more and more yearningly to the day when we shall see this, as well as take it for granted. For yourself I am in less apprehension; for I know that if you are spared, you will not die a member of the Church of Rome." His prophecy held true; the friend came back to the Anglican communion. But his critics thought Robertson much too lenient with others who did not return. They suspected that he had caught the Roman fever.

Privately answering these charges, he explained that he had studied the "patristic system," and had no doubt that it offered peace to anyone who could believe in it. But his Scottish blood would have no such thing. Rome and High Churchism held peculiar attractions for those who craved awe, tenderness, and mystery in worship. Robertson felt that this esthetic appeal was too much for the cloister, too little for the market place. It enticed the senses. He did not want Christianity "droned away in litanies and frittered into genuflexions," to the neglect of the living present that weltered daily around him. He believed that the best Christianity thrives in exposure. Others could rest in peace, gazing wistfully at the past glories of the Church, lulling conscience in the "cloud region" of the spirit, and reflecting on the meditative charm of tracery in stone, chanting, dim religious light, the twinkle of candles, and the prickling odor of incense.

But not Robertson. He declared: "I would rather live solitary on the most desolate crag, shivering, with all the warm wraps of falsehood stripped off, gazing after unfound truth . . . than sit comfortably on more inhabited spots, where others were warm in a faith which is true to them, but which is false to me."

XII

The Barbs of the Critics

HIS health had been poor, and through 1851 it became
still more troublesome. Not much of outward consequence
happened during the first six months of the year; but now
and then he burst out with some expression of ever-increasing
pain. He wrote to a friend, excusing himself for not having
prepared the customary notes for his sermons; he had not
been equal to the task. A short while before he had preached
on "The Three Crosses on Calvary," in which he said: "No
one can know what suffering is till he has known mental
torture; and no one can know the extremity of corporeal
suffering till, like his Master, he has counted the long hours
of torture one by one, and through night after night has
heard the clock strike in protracted anguish. This is what
we are called upon to endure, and then often it is that fret-
fulness and impatience break across our souls, and we wish
that the whole of our future could be concentrated into one
sharp hour."

Worn in mind as well as in body, Robertson read "next to
nothing." Yet his overstrained intellect was not tearing out
his life so much as the consuming fire of his emotions. He
wanted to live; he knew now that his work would not be done
so long as God had anything for him to suffer. "Last night,
till dawn today, suffering kept me awake, gnashing my teeth,

or rather setting them, like poor Prometheus, in defiance of
the vulture's beak. Only my vulture was feeding on my
cerebellum, and digging its talons in a most uncivil way into
the organs of emotionness, philoprogenitiveness, obstinacy,
etc., etc., leaving the nobler organs free." His greatest victories came not on the battlefield of which he once had
dreamed; they were silent victories won in manly endurance,
in humility, and in reliance of the soul upon God.

In 1851 Robertson began the lectures from Paul's letters
to the Corinthians. These he continued until his last illness.
His final message in Trinity Chapel came from the last chapter of the second epistle. He chose Corinthians for many
reasons, principally because the ancient church in Corinth
resembled the church in Brighton, surrounded by a bewildering civilization, setting forth prejudices, and quarreling over
secondary issues. First and Second Corinthians were not
altogether argumentative, like Romans, nor did they center
like Galatians in a single doctrine. Posing a multitude of
questions, these Corinthian letters gave Robertson a wide
range of topics. The truths of Paul still held, and applied
to Brighton fully as much as to Corinth. The preacher declared, "Religion is life, and right instruction in religion
is not the investigation of obsolete and curious doctrines,
but the application of spiritual principles to the questions,
and modes of action, which concern present existence, in the
market, the shop, the study, and the street."

Social action still captivated Robertson's thoughts. He
hoped that the Church would become a society of men united
in one another, because united in God. But he foretold a new
tyranny if laborers, successful in their reforms, turned their
new instruments of power toward selfish ends. The struggle
of a far-off generation would be to break them down: "They

will be the bloated aristocrats of the year 2000, and the chivalry of that age will be exhibited in a crusade against them." He cared little for the advancement of the race, if that meant only some future paradise in which mortals could eat, drink, sleep, and fully indulge their appetites, trying to glut themselves with enjoyments that perish in the handling.

In this guise civilization would become a Frankenstein's monster, a wretched, living corpse. Writing to a friend in 1851, Robertson expressed his repugnance of much that went by the name of progress. "A Lord Mayor's feast is a manifestation, and a very material one, of large resources, great contrivance, and aldermanic intellect. . . . Multiply the alderman's paradise by the accumulated science of a thousand years, and I do not think it proves us a bit nearer the conversion of this earth into a kingdom of God. . . . The invention of piquant sauces, luxurious furniture, tasteful jewelry, etc., etc., etc., I humbly decline to accept as proofs of anything beyond the fact that man is a very sagacious and surprising beaver. A spirit? *Non, mille fois non*, unless he can show something more than this."

Such was his frame of thought in the summer of 1851 when the Prince Consort's Great Exhibition opened at the Crystal Palace, London. Here the nations of the world displayed their finest wares. The Exhibition symbolized the era of expansion, infinite possibilities, and the growth of all sciences and arts "from more to more." As Robertson walked beneath the shining acres of glass he realized that he was not a "productive" member of society. Later in the year he said from his pulpit: "No man could have stood last summer in that structure where all the works of man were exhibited in one place, without hoping great things for the human race." Yet he did not let his expectations run wild. Scientists could shape and reshape the resources of nature. But what man could distill selfishness from the human heart?

Working men from every part of Great Britain converged on London for the Exhibition. Some churchmen, accordingly, arranged a series of summer lectures. Mr. Drew, of St. John's Church on Fitzroy Square, asked various ministers to preach. Two of the outstanding names were Kingsley and Maurice, Anglican clergymen known for their social passion. Robertson, less well known, also received an invitation. He was not closely allied with these other men. In the spring of 1851 Maurice visited for perhaps an hour with the younger minister in Brighton. "Maurice, gentlemanly and calm, about fifty years of age, spoke less than I did. I was ashamed to feel that I had the talking to myself, and learned nothing except a lesson of humility." Maurice said that he had been pleased with Robertson's published addresses to the working men. At that time, Robertson did not wish to take on the added burden of summer lectures.

But when summer came, Robertson went up to London. His subject was the story of Nabal and David, which he called "The Message of the Church to Men of Wealth." There was some criticism of the minister, of the sermon, and in fact, of the entire series. In the thick of it stood tall, ungainly Charles Kingsley. He preached on "the acceptable year of the Lord." After the sermon the rector of St. John's stood at his reading desk, and said: "I have a duty to perform—one of the most painful that has ever devolved upon me. . . . I feel compelled to say, that while much that the preacher has advanced has given me great satisfaction, I must and do protest against much that he has said as extremely imprudent and untrue. I may say, also, it is altogether different to what I had been led to expect."

Sounding the alarm of ecclesiastics, the newspapers declared that Kingsley and Maurice, and Robertson along with them, were socialistic. Although he differed from these other reformers in many ways, Robertson saw in them much that he admired. He said of Kingsley, "He may be more right than I think." True, Kingsley was rash. He was perhaps mistaken in his vehemence. But are there not times to use a scourge? Robertson exclaimed: "I wish to God we had a little soldier's spirit in our Church! No! the Church of England will endure no chivalry, no dash, no effervescing enthusiasm. . . . Well, I suppose God will punish us, if in no other way, by banishing from us all noble spirits, like Newman and Manning, in one direction, and men like Kingsley in another, leaving us to flounder in the mud of commonplace, unable to rise or sink above the dead level. Day by day my hopes are sinking. We dare not say the things we feel. Who can? Who possibly may, when *Records, Guardians,* brother ministers, and lay hearers are ready at every turn to call out heterodoxy?"

The newspaper that most frequently and violently attacked Robertson was the *Record,* the blatant voice of the Evangelical party. The editors dipped their pens in gall and acid. When there was a chance to call a minister bad names, the *Record* equaled the opportunity. For a long while the paper had been sniping at Robertson, but as the circle of his influence began to spread, they opened a barrage. "They are beginning to think me of sufficient importance to be put down." Robertson noted that his fellow victims were Maurice and Archdeacon Hare, Donaldson, the classical scholar, and the poet Tennyson. "Pretty good society; and, to borrow an expression of poor Shelley, 'I would rather be damned with such men than saved with the *Record.*'"

He wrote to Mr. Drew, the clergyman who had invited him to preach in London: "I have just had sent me the *Record*, in which your letter appears, and thank you heartily for the generous defense of me which it contains. The *Record* has done me the honour to abuse me for some time past, for which I thank them gratefully. God forbid they should ever praise me! One number alone contained four unscrupulous lies about me, on no better evidence than that some one had told them, who had been told by somebody else. They shall have no disclaimer from me. If the *Record* can put a man down, the sooner he is put down the better. The only time I have ever said anything about Socialism in the pulpit has been to preach against it. The Evangelicalism (so-called) of the *Record* is an emasculated cur, snarling at all that is better than itself, cowardly, lying and slanderous."

Sharp words! In the pulpit of Trinity Chapel, Robertson sometimes mentioned party journals and reviews. Each one branded the others as unchristian. Their narrow molds of thought teemed with rancor. Robertson declared in all seriousness, and with no theatrical anger: "I am not asking you what are the views maintained—whether Evangelical, Anglican, or Romish—but what is the spirit of that fountain from which the religious life of so many is nourished? . . . The spirit which guides the 'religious press' of this country— which dictates those personalities, which prevents controversialists from seeing what is good in their opponents, which attributes low motives to account for excellent lives, and teaches men whom to suspect and shun, rather than point out where it is possible to admire and love—is a spirit 'set on fire of hell.' "

Unfortunately Robertson sometimes charged the Evangelicals as a group with the debits of the *Record*. Like the prophet Elijah, his most signal failure occurred at the strong point of his character. The strength and weakness of Robertson was intensity. In preaching it became his power; in criticism, his failing. He had a robust but not an ugly temper; he did not lash out from spite, revenge, or the desire to wound. Yet in dealing with the Evangelicals he was more than outspoken. What irritated him was the exchange of God's immeasurable and incomprehensible love for a handful of maxims. Forgive seven times? Christ said seventy times seven! That was no maxim; it was a heart principle—one that Robertson struggled to apply to the Evangelicals.

When these folk began to prate about salvation for a small number of the elect, meaning themselves, Robertson could not help becoming angry. He looked for some surprises on the Day of Judgment. Protestantism, he said, referring especially to the Evangelicals, "comes with its parchment 'signed, sealed, and delivered,' making over heaven to you by a legal bond, gives its receipt in full, makes a debtor and creditor account, clears up the whole by a most business-like arrangement. . . . And when this Shylock-like affair with the scales and weights is concluded, it bids you be sure that the most rigorous justice and savage cruelty can want no more. Whereupon Selfishness shrewdly casts up the account, and says, 'Audited! I am safe.' "

For individuals in the Evangelical party, however, he had a deep attachment. If he did not relish their dogma, he knew that his friends often proved better than their creed, and their hearts sounder than their heads. He owed most of his love for the Bible to his Evangelical parents. He had learned the secret of effective preaching from Evangelical ministers. He admired Lord Shaftesbury and other leaders of the

Evangelical movement. Even at this time, he was writing confidentially about doctrine to an Evangelical pastor near by. As for the ladies of the party, whatever their faults, they did feed the hungry and cut out garments for the un- clad. They recognized a rule of goodness higher than the opinion of their neighbors. If they reserved the mansions of heaven too largely for themselves, yet they believed that the kingdom was for those who put their trust in God.

Their danger and often their failing was mechanization. They had bolted down their thoughts. In extreme cases, the Evangelicals valued the printed Word of God more than the Living Voice that breaks into the solitude of conscience. They worshiped the Bible rather than the God of the Bible. They lived very largely according to a memorized system. Robertson therefore objected:

"I complain of Evangelicalism because it tries to explain the Atonement by Reason—a debtor's and creditor's ac- count. As to the desire after breadth and comprehension, that I confess. I am sick of hatred, suspicion, slander, and condemnation of one another, and long to believe in men's good rather than in their evil, in God rather than in the devil. I believe I hold 'the distinctive features of my religion' sharply enough, too sharply for a great many people; but I cannot and will not judge those who do not hold them as I do; nay, I go further, I will not cease trying to love them and believing that, under other words, they often express the truths that I hold most dear.

"To the question, 'Who is my neighbor?' I reply, as my Master did, by the example that He gave, 'The alien and the heretic.' And I do not think that He will say my charity is too large, or my inclusiveness too great. Alas! alas! when I see Romanists cursing the Church of England, Evangeli-

cals shaking their heads about the Christianity of Tractarians, Tractarians banning Dissenters, Dissenters anathe-
matising Unitarians, and Unitarians of the old school
condemning the more spiritual of the new; I am forced to
hope that there is more inclusiveness in the Love of God than
in the bitter orthodoxy of sects and churches."

Robertson believed that he could never become an Evangelical, a Roman Catholic, or an infidel. He was too much
of an individual to slide along the grooves of party thought.
He satisfied no party, for he belonged to none. Yet no smudge
of pride came to light in his standing apart. Not because
of stubbornness, not because of scoffing at what others believed, but because of the sheer massiveness of his thinking
he was bound to stand alone. To him the tragedy of the age
was that religious leaders mistook their enemy. They could
argue over tittles while in other places men were debating
the very existence of God.

"Is it opposition to sensuality, to pride, to vice, to evil
generally?—or is it opposition to some doctrine held by
this or that section of the Christian world? . . . Let me
bring this more closely home to you, and earnestly entreat
the members of this congregation to sever themselves from
that bitter spirit of controversy which is tearing asunder
Christian society in this town. My Christian brethren, if
Christ be your Master, what in this world is your foe? Not
Tractarianism nor Dissent, neither Popery nor Evangelicalism. These may be more or less forms of error; but they who
hold them are your brethren, battling against the same evil
that you are."

For the most part Robertson had been, in Southey's
phrase, bigoted only against bigots; toward the end of his
life he learned the hardest lesson of all, in his own words

to "tolerate even intolerance." He strove to become more like the One "who, when He was reviled, reviled not again; when He suffered He threatened not; but committed Himself to Him that judgeth righteously." The year 1851 was as arduous and burdensome as the ones that had gone before; it was aggravated by criticism, and made doubly miserable by the sharpening pain of disease. Autumn came, and winter. On December 28 Robertson preached on "The Transitoriness of Life."

"And now has come winter again. This is the last Sunday of the year. It is not a mere preacher's voice performing an allotted task. The call and the correspondence are real. . . . We have all felt it in the damp mist, in the slanting shadows, the dimmer skies, the pale, watery glow of the red setting sun, shorn of half its lustre. In the dripping of the woodland, in the limp leaves trodden by heaps into clay, in the depressing north wind, in the sepulchral cough of the aged man at the corner of the street, under the inclement sky, God has said to us, as He said to Moses, 'Pause, and number thy days, for they are numbered.'"

XIII

The Minister with the Poets

ROBERTSON was an old man at thirty-six, and for some reason that he did not fully understand, still alive. Throughout 1852 he kept working as hard as ever. Earlier he had promised to give a lecture to help the working men's organization. The members had struggled through a tangled year. Robertson labored tirelessly to make their endeavor a success. He had written in November that he was "at working men's meetings and lectures every evening." Then came the plea for him to give a public speech. The secretary presented Robertson with a formal invitation, which he accepted: "I am very unfit at present for the excitement of addressing numbers; but knowing that the insufficiency will be pardoned, and feeling deep interest in the success of the working men, I shall not allow this to stand in the way."

For a topic he chose "The Influence of Poetry on the Working Classes." The arts of language lay close to Robertson's thought. On Sunday he never spouted long passages of verse from the pulpit; the longest quotation in his sermons consists of four lines. He rarely fell into the routine phrase, "As Shakespeare says . . ." But he lived with the poets at his elbow. Sometimes he repeated snatches of their

153

song, or gave the gist of a passage, or echoed a rhythm or mood or thought. These drift phrases appeared in his sermons: "Conscience does make cowards"; "lov'd I not honour more"; "dim religious light"; "he prayeth well who loveth well"; "getting and spending"; "broken lights."

Probably he slipped these into his speech hardly aware that he was quoting; for he had lived with Shakespeare, Lovelace, and Milton, with Coleridge, Wordsworth, and Tennyson, until their words fit inextricably into the pattern of his thought. He scattered random lines of Gray's "Elegy" through his sermons: "Beneath those rugged elms, that yew-tree's shade"; "the paths of glory lead but to the grave"; "long-drawn aisle and fretted vault"; "rod of empire"; "the genial current of the soul"; and one line that must have meant more to him than all the rest, "Melancholy marked him for her own." His sermons could be trawled again and again, every time with a new catch of poetic phrases. "The Influence of Poetry on the Working Classes" represented the gradually ripened thought of his living among the English poets.

The two lectures came in February, 1852. Each of the audiences numbered more than a thousand. Robertson spoke extempore. He variously defined poetry as the natural utterance of excited feeling; the language of symbolism; imagination wrought into form by art; and the indirect expression of feelings that cannot be expressed directly. He said that science destroys poetry, but that the burning heart can bring poetry out of science again, "asserting a wonder and a vague mystery of life and feeling beneath and beyond all science," and discovering mysterious beauty in the commonplace.

Turning from science to natural beauty, Robertson

thought once again of the Alps. There every sound and sight
added to an impression of unity: the slow wreathing of mist
around the summits, the plunge of the vulture into the valley,
the scattered flight of birds surprised at a feast of carrion;
and over all the brooding of a storm, the lightning flash,
and muttering thunder. Robertson remembered feelings,
"which in their fulness man can feel but once in life; mingled
sensations of awe and triumph, and defiance of danger, pride,
rapture, contempt of pain, humbleness and intense repose,
as if all the strife and struggle of the elements were only
uttering the unrest of man's bosom; so that in all such scenes
there is a feeling of relief, and he is tempted to cry out ex-
ultingly, 'There! there! all this was in my heart, and it was
never said out till now!' "

But why poetry for workmen who seldom traveled a fur-
long from the town in which they were born? Robertson
said that all men "feel, weep, laugh, alike: alike have their
aspiring and their degraded moods: that which tells on one
human spirit, tells also upon another." What he said belonged to men of work, not particularly, but as humans. If
verse influenced men in the least, it should influence working
men. Not all the poetry was in the Alps; it came to light in
ordinary things. Tennyson found it in a crumpled poppy,
Wordsworth in "nutting," and Burns in a mouse. Even
Brighton, treeless and prosaic, lay beneath the illimitable
sky,

> . . . Without bound
> Without dimension, where length, breadth, and height
> And time and place are lost.

Though one did not have the tongue of a poet, said Robertson, he "might have watched with delight, beyond all words,

last night, the long, deep purple lines of cloud, edged with intolerable radiance, passing into orange, yellow, pale green, and leaden blue, and reflected below in warm, purple shadows, and cold, green lights, upon the sea—and then, the dying of it all away."

Not only should the workman enjoy the finest poetry, and marvel at the golden splendor out of the west. He should write. He should become a poet. Men of letters in England had been either gentlemen by birth, or else had accepted the tradition that looked down on mechanical skills. But Robertson prophesied: "The poetry of the coming age must come from the working classes. . . . Men of work! we want our poetry from you. . . . Now rise and tell us the living meaning there may be in the smoke of manufactories, and the heroism of perseverance, and the poetry of invention, and the patience of uncomplaining resignation." It is remarkable that in the early nineteenth century there had been little good prose and even less good verse about machinery, and that railroads, factories, and the like, should have prompted so little imaginative writing. Robertson was one of the few men of the time who sensed the poetry of steel and steam.

In these lectures Robertson mentioned the recent war scare. In 1848 *Punch* had carried articles and cartoons on an expected French invasion of Brighton; and now again in 1852 the policy of Napoleon III aroused alarm in England. There were rumblings of a universal war. In a letter Robertson said that he thought the war inevitable; everywhere men were foreboding it. He expressed the hope that in the coming conflict of nations, "America and England will stand side by side, instead of opposite; for, if not, it will be all over for the cause of liberty, for some centuries at least. . . . Strange, that people with so much to lose in case of war should be so blindly unwilling to pay in the present for the means of peace!" Yet in his lectures on poetry he gave the fullest expression to his military ideal.

Poetry discerns the redeeming nobleness in the shambles of war. Robertson told of a British cavalry charge against a robber tribe of India. Eleven Britishers attacked seventy Indians at the crest of a steep mountain. One after another the assailants fell. There was a custom among the hillsmen, when one of their chieftains died in battle, to bind his wrist with a thread of red or green, the red being the higher honor. When the British found the gashed bodies of their dead comrades, twined round the wrist of every soldier was the crimson thread.

Robertson ended with a challenge to the French army that threatened invasion of England: "If a foreign foot be planted on our sacred soil—if the ring of the rifle of the Chasseurs de Vincennes be heard upon these shores, terrible as the first reverses might be, when discipline could be met only by raw enthusiasm . . . they may yet chance to learn that British chivalry did not breathe her last at Moodkee, or Ferozeshah, or Sobraon, or Goojerat, or Meeanee, or Hyaderabad. They may yet be taught that there is something beyond the raw hysterics of a transient excitement in the spirit of self-sacrifice which we have learned from our Master's Cross. They may yet discover that amongst the artisans, and peasants, and working men of England, there are a thousand thousand worthy to be brothers of those heroic eleven who sleep beneath the rocks of Trukkee, with the red thread of honour round their wrists."

The speech was published, and received high praise. Henry Drummond, commending Robertson on the lectures, said: "I have received your essay with many thanks. It appears to me that you are the only person who is grappling with the natural infidelity of minds educated in everything except religion." Robertson forwarded the letter to a friend and remarked: "Mr. Drummond's letter is interesting, inasmuch as it exhibits a deeper perception of what I was aiming at than I have yet seen in any one. To produce a belief in the reality of invisible Truth and Beauty is the chief end of my insignificant work here."

Lord Carlisle sent a congratulatory letter, along with a copy of his own volume of "Lectures on Pope." Robertson answered at once: "I will not allow a post to pass without thanking you for your kind present and kinder note, the approval of which I feel to be very invigorating. I was very glad to find that there was not a syllable of the 'Lectures on Pope' which jarred with my estimate of him, which I a little feared. . . . My sentence, 'The best poetry demands study as severe as mathematics require,' is very justly open to criticism, but more, I think, from the unfinished abruptness of the phraseology than from its real meaning. The best poetry has a sense which is level to the apprehension at once; not being obscure in expression, nor metaphysical or scholastic in thought; but then any one who had caught this meaning at the first glance would be greatly mistaken if he supposed that he had got all, or nearly all, it meant. . . . In the graceful courtesy with which your lordship acknowledges that there is 'some identity of view between us,' I receive the best and most cheering reward that my little pamphlet has obtained."

The lectures on poetry not only gave new life to the working men's organization, renamed the Mechanics' Institution, but raised funds to see them past their troubles. Soon after the lectures, Robertson visited again in Cheltenham. At Christchurch the familiar hymns and the tones of the organ went home, and for a while it seemed that he had never been away. But the years, though few, had wrought a change among the people. Many of the old places were empty or else filled by others. Wrinkles and gray hair had visibly increased. Young men and women, whom he had known as boys and girls, came to him and asked, "Don't you remember me?"

If the people had changed, the hills around Cheltenham had not. They looked as beautiful as ever. Robertson tramped with his brother, Struan, through the woods, and along what he called "some of the loveliest valleys I know anywhere." The more he saw of the countryside, the more its loveliness struck him. He said of the hills that girded Cheltenham: "In all probability part of the beauty of scenery depends upon your knowing all the points far and near, so that imagination assists the eye very much, and you supply what you know to what you see, fancying all the time that you see it."

He knew these hills by heart; he had once prepared here for the army. Here, too, he had gone riding with Mrs. Robertson in the early days of their marriage. He had been a daring horseman, whose skill excited admiration. One day, while riding with his wife and some friends, he put his horse to a lofty hedge. It was a dangerous leap; the horse balked. He tried again and again. At last the horse cleared the hedge, coming down on the other side with a crash, his rider under him. Robertson picked himself up with a smile. On the present visit he rode once more into the country with his brother and Mr. Munro. They passed the scenes of many a desperate leap that he and his brother had taken years before.

Mr. Munro said, "Why, Robertson, the farmers would not know you again, you ride so quietly."

"I have been thinking several times during the ride, as I looked at a tempting wall or gate, of that line of Byron's applied to one who has spent his force, and was unmoved by Beauty; 'But now it moved him as it moves the wise.'" He took a single leap to show that it was still in him, if he wished. But all of that day, as during most of the visit, he felt depressed and low.

In Cheltenham Robertson visited Alfred Tennyson, whose "In Memoriam" he considered "the most precious work published in this century." A large segment of the recent lectures on poetry Robertson had given to a discussion of this work. His admiration for Tennyson, however, was more than literary. The two men had known each other in 1846–47 when both lived at Cheltenham. Hallam Tennyson said that Robertson was "much beloved" of his father. There was a little room atop the house on St. James' Square in which the two probably discussed literature. Here Tennyson, pipe in mouth, surrounded by papers and books in glorious disarray, would talk more freely than anywhere else "on men and things and what death means."

Tennyson was a Christian. He did not often speak of religion, though he sometimes said that Christianity was tugging at his heart. His son, Hallam, remembered his father's saying: "The first time I met Robertson I felt that he expected something notable from me because I knew that he admired my poems, that he wished to pluck the heart from my mystery; so for the life of me from pure nervousness I could talk of nothing but beer." As the acquaintance deepened, Robertson, though the younger of the two, had strong

influence over the man of letters. Tennyson considered his
friend the most spiritual of all the preachers of the century,
and as his own religious ideas took form, he became in his
independent way a follower of Robertson.

When Robertson went back to Brighton, he did so re-
luctantly. "I feel as low as a schoolboy going back to school
which he dislikes. I had not time to call on Tennyson." In
Brighton he had other friends who participated in his
literary interests. One of these, Lady Byron, showed him
some of her husband's manuscripts. She was many years
Robertson's senior, but they were close friends, having known
each other almost from the time of his coming to Trinity
Chapel. Lady Byron stood out as one of the noblest women
he had ever met, though on occasion she had a whim of iron,
and could be not altogether undeserving of her poet-
husband's thrust:

> Serenely purest of her sex that live,
> But wanting one sweet weakness—to forgive.

For all that, Robertson said, "Her calm, subdued character, warm sympathy, and manifold wisdom have been one of
my greatest privileges here." She told him the sacred con-
fidences of her life. Had she not outlived Robertson, he
would no doubt have edited memoirs and letters that she en-
trusted to him. He paid visits to her homes at Brighton and
Esher, attended the deathbed of her daughter, heard her
plans for the grandchildren, and encouraged her charities,
which included a training home for girls and one of the first
industrial schools in England. He helped her with her business affairs. "I have consulted lawyers on matters of difficulty," she said, "but Robertson seemed better able to give

me advice." She called her pastor "the lone, the unrevealed," and honored him as the best of all the preachers she had ever known or heard.

Once again, in August of 1852, Robertson promised to lecture in Brighton. The invitation came from the members of the Athenaeum, a literary club that had repeatedly asked the minister to favor them with a public address. He thought of speaking on "The Influence of Fiction." With Dickens, Thackeray, Charlotte Brontë and George Eliot, Trollope, Kingsley, Meredith, and others, all of whom wrote in the "fifties," the English novel was entering its golden age. Another idea, however, had been growing in Robertson's mind. He wished to pay tribute to William Wordsworth, who had died in 1850. In Robertson's estimation Wordsworth was more than a versifier; he was a preacher who interpreted God to man, and a prophet whom God had set as a beacon in a stormy time. The minister decided to speak on the life and poetry of Wordsworth. The lecture gradually took shape through the next six months.

Because of some difficulties about getting a room, the Athenaeum postponed the lecture. But in February, a year after "The Influence of Poetry on the Working Classes," Robertson made final preparations to give the address. "I have no journals of books read, or thoughts matured to send you; for my whole journal has been thinking,—thinking— thinking about Wordsworth. I wish I had written the lecture, but I had not time; it takes so long in the mere act of penmanship. It is all in my brain somehow or other; whether it will come out orderly or tremblingly, I do not know. Then there is the question whether health or strength will be such as to give a command of words, and these two questions make the whole experiment a hazardous one. However, I must shut my eyes and harden my heart, as they say to boys riding over their first leap. When you get this it will all be over."

Robertson wished to stress three points: the appreciation of poetry in general, and of Wordsworth in particular; the character and life of the poet as they bore on his art; and the theories and poetic principles of Wordsworth, "how far they are true, how far they have been exaggerated, and how far Wordsworth himself worked out the principles he has laid down." Obviously Robertson thought the last of these most important; in fact it was *the* subject. He handled so much material in the first two divisions that he put aside the third for another lecture, which, owing to his health, he never gave.

In the first place, he said, the public knew almost nothing about Wordsworth. While almost everyone had heard his name, relatively few understood the man or his writings. The usual conception of the poet was something on this order: "An old man who lived somewhere in the Lake districts, who raved considerably of Lake scenery, who wrote a large number of small poems, all of them innocent, many of them puerile and much laughed at, at the time they appeared, by clever men; that they were lashed in the reviews, and annihilated by Lord Byron, as, for instance, in those well-known lines:—

> A drowsy, frowsy poem, called Excursion
> Writ in a manner which is my aversion;

and that he was guilty of a vast mass of other verses, all exceedingly innocent, and at the same time exceedingly dull and heavy."

This false impression Robertson sets out to correct. He says that the first requirement to understand Wordsworth is unworldliness. Like the child in the sublime "Ode to Immortality," one must keep something of heaven lying about him still, as he moves continually between the two worlds of the visible and the invisible. A man whose life is choked by worldliness simply cannot understand the highest poetry. Further, true feelings must be trained and disciplined by nature. Stagnant minds at sixty years of age think of poetry as they did in adolescence; elegance of language and the pomp of rhythm seem to be the highest standards. But should not the elderly man have a firmer appreciation of poetic beauty than the youth? The discipline of feeling should go on year by year.

Any wiseacre who reads Wordsworth to catch flaws or to write parodies will find grist for his mill. Only the person who thinks and feels with the poet will profit by Wordsworth; only one who walks with him "in gentleness of heart" will find the grandeur of his simplicity. "No man needs this discipline and preparation more than the student of Wordsworth, for he gives to us the subtle and pure and delicate and refined succession of human feelings, of which the mind is scarcely conscious, except at the moment when the figure is before us, and we are listening with stilled breath to the mysterious march of our inner life." The poetry of Wordsworth is uneventful, unadorned, and unmannered; it is "like listening to the mysterious music in the conch sea shell, which is so delicate and refined that we are uncertain whether it is the music and sound of the shell, or merely the pulses throbbing in our own ear; it is like watching the quivering rays of fleeting light that shoot up to heaven as we are looking at the sunset."

The audience seemed appreciative but restrained, inasmuch as the thought was deep, and Robertson used no claptrap, which any practiced speaker can easily fabricate. "One

line to tell you that my lecture went off last night successfully
—that is, I did not break down, and preserved self-possession
throughout; the room a perfect cram, and hundreds went
away; but I have been suffering from severe pain in the head
ever since—shooting thrills so sharp and sudden that I can
scarcely forbear an exclamation. Whether people liked it or
not, I do not know; and if I could only get rid of these stabs
in the brain every ten minutes, I should not care. Two lights
with reflectors were placed on the table, glaring in my face
all the time, which prevented my seeing anybody. There was
little or no applause, except now and then a low murmur;
but, on the whole, I was glad of this, for the worst acknowl-
edgment that can be made of an instructive lecture is to clap,
and I think they showed their good taste."

The *South Church Union*, a High Church paper, issued
an editorial against Robertson. For once he answered in
print. He stated his reason thus: if he never defended himself, many would begin to think him incapable of defense.
The editor charged that he had been trumpeting pantheistic
thought, and opposing the High Church. Actually Robertson had said that the pantheist tended "to see the god-like
everywhere, the personal God nowhere." On the other hand,
he went on to say, the High Churchman tended to hedge in
Deity with consecrated churches and consecrated days, consecrated ritual and consecrated priests. Robertson tried to
show that the tendency is not always the error; and that
many sincere High Churchmen, like Wordsworth, saw in
these places, times, acts, and persons "a sanctity only rela-
tive, and not intrinsic."

Emphatically denying that he had spoken treason against
the High Church movement, Robertson answered: "I do not
merely say that I was not guilty of this paltry work. I say it

is simply impossible to me. To affirm, whatever may be taught by our savage polemics, whether Tractarian or Evangelical, that the new commandment is NOT this—'that ye hate one another,' and that discipleship to Christ is proved more by the intensity of love for good than by the vehemence of bitterness against error, is with me a desire too deep, too perpetual, and too unsatisfied to have allowed the possibility of my joining even for one moment in the cowardly cry with which the terrors and the passions of the half-informed are lashed by platform rhetoric into hatred of High Churchism."

XIV

The Death of Robertson

BETWEEN "The Influence of Poetry on the Working Classes" and the "Lecture on Wordsworth," in April, 1852, the young men of Robertson's congregation asked permission to give their minister a testimonial. They invited him to a tea at the Town Hall. Nearly one hundred men signed an address that told of their gratitude for his unwearied labors. Clerks, shop assistants, servants, and others of their class whom Robertson had helped, and who did not know how else to say what was in their hearts, added their names to the document in witness of their affection. One of their number, Mr. Evans, gave the address. With deep earnestness he touched on the benefits that every one of them had received from the ministry of Robertson, whose reconciling work, straightforwardness, and devotion to the young men of Brighton, had made Christianity real to them. There could have been no higher praise.

As Robertson did not know the contents of the address beforehand, he did not prepare a definite reply. He could simply speak from the fullness of his heart. All rose as he began; when he finished there were cheers. "We are not here to bandy compliments with one another. You have not come to flatter me: and I have not come, with any affected coyness, to pretend to disclaim your flattery, in order that it

167

may be repeated. You have told me, in the frank spirit of Englishmen, that my ministry has done you good. Frankly, as an Englishman, I tell you with all my heart, I do believe it. I know that there are men who once wandered in darkness and doubt, and could find no light, who have now found an anchor, and a rock, and resting-place. I know that there are men who were feeling bitterly and angrily, what seemed to them the unfair differences of society, who now regard them in a gentler, more humble, and more tender spirit. I know that there are rich who have been led to feel more generously towards the poor. I know that there are poor who have been taught to feel more truly and more fairly towards the rich.

"I *believe*—for on such a point *God* can only *know*—that there are men who have been induced to place before themselves a higher standard, and perhaps I may venture to add, have conformed their lives more truly to that standard. I dare not hide my belief in this. I am deeply grateful in being able to say that, if my ministry were to close tomorrow, it would not have been in this town at least altogether a failure."

Even so, the satisfaction of the hour was tinged with sadness. The end had drawn nearer than any of his friends could realize. He was weary; he was in pain. "In the midst of the homage of a crowd, I felt alone, and as if friendless"; but he also said, "at least whenever I feel strongly, I make it a rule now to assume the probability that physical causes have something to do with the matter." Robertson's study became languid and miserable. He set his face like a flint to prepare a sermon. Every thought was an agony. "It reminds me of the 'Song of the Shirt'—'work, work, work;' and the perpetual treadmill necessity of being ever ready twice a week with earnest thoughts on solemn subjects is a task which is quite enough to break down all originality, and convert a racehorse into a dray." Whatever he did exhausted him. "Therefore, if in this anything sounds harsh or misanthropic, think it is not I, but one of the azure demons whose property I myself am for the nonce."

Indeed, he had nearly worn himself out. In an expository lecture on Corinthians, Robertson left part of a chapter to explain, "*if God permit*, next Sunday." It was as much as he could do to prepare a morning and an afternoon sermon every week; sometimes he failed even in that. More than once he had to fall back on his old stock of sermons. "John's Rebuke of Herod," which he gave in the spring of 1853, had been one of his messages in Cheltenham years before. Then, too, his manner of preaching changed. He often relied on a manuscript. He confessed his loss of power. "Today I have done little. Titus would have written, 'I have lost a day.' I prepared for Sunday with little zest and much lassitude of mind, walked with S——, read the newspaper, and scarcely anything else besides. It is strange how much more loss I feel in me of life's vital force than a year or two ago; it seems a tortoise existence; the truth of which simile you will appreciate, if you remember that the pulse of that creature beats about once to twenty pulsations of our blood, and every function of his nature, walking, etc., is performed in the slowest way, as if existence were dragged out."

The day following a long walk on the downs, he wrote, "I have been spending my time in laborious idleness—every thought I think, and every line I write or read, costing pain, sometimes acute, and sometimes dull, of brain. I shall not be able to go on much longer if this continues; whole tracts of brain seem to be losing their faculty, and becoming quite torpid and impotent—memory being the most observable and the most tormenting. All originating power I have ceased to try to exercise, on principle, lest it should go entirely."

Acid lines of suffering etched their way into his face. When he spoke there were marks of tension, cutting across the lines of those deeper and more abiding cares that did not change with the expression of the moment. His face belonged to one who had pushed beyond his limit, and aged beyond his years. Not long after the lecture on Wordsworth, while he was walking down a Brighton street with Julian Young, a bewildering pain stabbed him. His head grew dizzy, his eyes dimmed, he sank down into a black pool, and his body seemed to dissolve in its darkness.

Mr. Young carried him with difficulty into a near-by cobbler's shop. There was no furniture, so that he laid Robertson on the floor, and leaving him in the care of the shopkeeper, ran to a chemist's for salts and sal-volatile. When Young returned, Robertson lay still unconscious; perhaps fifteen minutes later he came to. Young urged him to ride home in a carriage, but said that "he expressed such determined repugnance to indulging in such effeminacy, as he called it, that I was compelled to yield to his wishes, and slowly escort him home on foot. On the road, he leant so heavily on my arm, and dragged his legs along with such difficulty, that I feared every moment that he would fall."

On arriving at the home, Young persuaded Robertson to rest in a chair, and to prop his feet on another. "I had repeatedly expostulated with him on his disregard to bodily health, urging on him the necessity of letting his over-wrought and over-cropped brain lie fallow for some time; for the meagreness of his appetite, the wakefulness of his nights, and the nervous pallor of his tongue, I thought were ugly symptoms." But to all Young's pleas and warnings,

Robertson answered, "Yes; you only tell me what my medical advisers confirm."

Young remarked, "I wish I could frighten you."

With a sad smile, Robertson admitted that he had often endured extreme pains at the back of his head. He had never thought them of any danger, since he had never suffered in the anterior lobes of the brain. But he had recently been undeceived on that point. Possibly Robertson fainted more than once; but probably he was describing the incident with Young when he wrote to another friend: "My first sensation, on coming to myself, was that of being conscious of voices around me, and I knew instantly that a crowd had gathered, though I had not in that hundredth part of a second opened my eyes. They tell me I leaped to my feet as if shot: I went a few steps into a shop, and fainted quite off into unconsciousness a second time; then came intense pain in the back of the head, which lasted for three hours. However, to avoid making a sensation, I went out to dinner, keeping my engagement; but it saved me nothing, for the fact is duly pilloried in the *Brighton Gazette* this morning, and my bell has rung with inquiries half-a-dozen times already."

On the advice of physicians, he went to Cheltenham for a rest. During his absence of three weeks Lady Byron and a number of other admirers raised a sum of two hundred pounds, in order to engage a curate for Robertson. He accepted their generosity and nominated a personal friend, the Rev. Ernest Tower. This gentleman was thoroughly industrious and deeply attached to Robertson. He called the Brighton preacher "the most faultless clergyman I have ever known." Their talents followed different channels, so that there would have been little danger of collision. As the curate was to preach the afternoon sermon, Robertson hoped to have more time for pastoral work. Apparently the arrangement satisfied the members of Trinity Chapel, as well as the two ministers.

But the Vicar of Brighton, who had a grudge against Mr. Tower, held the power of veto. Prompt and firm in his decision, the vicar refused to confirm the nomination. There was nothing for Robertson to do but toil on as best he could. Naturally the veto stirred up feelings in Brighton, and not a little comment. Shortly after the Tower affair, Robertson gave his opinion of the ministry. "It is certainly the most quarrelsome of all professions in the matter of a blue or green window, prevenient moonshine, or a bishop's nightcap, and the most cowardly when once it comes to a matter of right and wrong—of what they saw and what they did not see. Unless *clergy, of the type I am alluding to*, are forced to serve in the army for five years previous to ordination, to make them men, 'let alone' gentlemen, I think the Church, as an establishment, had better be snuffed out."

In his last months at Trinity Chapel, Robertson exclaimed: "I do dislike Brighton, but it is my present sphere, and I must make the best of it. The ministry is nowhere a bed of roses; and if there were so delectable a spot, it is not open for me to change to instead of this. It is a wise man's duty to try to work within his limitations in the best way he can, and grumble as little as possible or else cut himself asunder at once from all restrictions and obligations, by giving up his sphere of work entirely. What makes it, too, all the more difficult in my case is, that I am a marked man: and whether it be notoriety or popularity, no one on whom others' eyes are fixed in affection, or in malicious watchfulness for a false step, can emancipate himself from the necessity of caution, or take his own will for his law, when Will merely means unbridled course of inclination. . . . Now I acknowledge I am not invulnerable to slanders—I know no one who is—nor am I a man to whom the world will accord impunity. Even in to-day's *Gazette* there is a long, vulgar, dull lampoon upon my views, which wretched and ignorant as it is, is yet irritating."

Fatigue and tension were terrible. The physical strain of his work proved too much. The preaching of masterly sermons, morning and afternoon on Sunday, the teaching of confirmation classes, the pastoral duties that he carried on despite weakness, the lectures on poetry, the turbulence of a controversy on Sabbath observance, the fury of Brighton elections, the difficulty with the vicar, the letter-writing that went on all the while at a ravishing pace—all these hastened the end. The marvel is not that he broke so soon, but that he lasted so long. Robertson consulted three London doctors, paid them three guineas, and heard their advice. The first ordered him to eat "some hash or other." The second predicted "organic collapse of the brain." The third recommended—"lettuce"! The Brighton physicians were scarcely more helpful. Dr. Taylor prescribed opiates, which Robertson once had thought an unmanly asylum from pain, but which he agreed to take in his last illness. Doctors Allen and Whitehouse frankly told him that his ailment lay beyond the reach of medicine.

Everyone in the congregation knew of the pastor's condition, and many urged on him favorite cures. A chemist who attended Trinity Chapel offered Robertson a battery so as to try the new cure of galvanism. "I called to thank him and decline the offer. But in conversation he persuaded me just to go and look at his apparatus. I took the ends of the wire, completing the circuit, and experienced the usual pleasurable tingling. Then holding it by one hand, and he holding the other wire in his, he touched the back of my head and neck, where I have lately felt pain and numbness. Not a sensation did it elicit, though the spot is generally, he says, most sensitive. Then he touched my forehead. It was but for a second. Instantly a crashing pain shot through as if my skull was stove in, and a bolt of fire were burning through and through. I sprang to my feet, stood for a second or two wild with pain, and then sank down, and should have had another lady-like swoon, if he had not run to the shop and fetched some poignant aromatic. He seemed much astonished, frightened, and perplexed at what had taken place. I was not surprised. I knew that something was wrong there."

The physicians diagnosed the trouble as an abscess of the cerebellum, complicated with symptoms of the heart. They admitted that they were powerless. Few, indeed, had any real hope that Robertson would recover. Likewise he felt the sentence of death within him. He was not sure how long his body would tarry. He might drag on for years, a burden to his family and a weariness to himself. By some power stronger than reason he knew that his pastoral work had come to an end. How much better to die than to lose all zest for the ministry, and to have no strength or impulse to undertake his duties! Death would be better than to watch the fire of his thought slowly dwindle to ashes. A voice spoke in the depths of his soul: "Your work is done."

"My life for the last few weeks has been one of perpetual pain—forced to work, and forced to mix with people, and to talk when it has taken me actually, only two days ago, an hour and a quarter to crawl, by back streets, from Kemp Town, in suffering all the way; and now at this moment langour makes me stop in writing after every third line. If my congregation had not come forward so generously, and if I had not received so many letters full of kindness, containing expression of pain and regret about my looks, etc., I should, I verily think, have given up work entirely, so hardly does it press upon me, and so much that is painful have I had to submit to. But their warmth has settled the question and left me no alternative, and I must work on as long as I have strength for it."

On the fifth of June, Robertson spoke for the last time at his chapel. In the morning he preached on behalf of the orphanage. In the afternoon he came to the closing chapter of Second Corinthians. Ironically, he chose for his text, "Finally, brethren, farewell." During the week he made painful efforts for his duties of the next Sunday, but the doctors told him what he already knew, that he was in no condition to preach. There were last-minute arrangements, and when the congregation gathered, they learned that their pastor would not be with them. Many feared that his text had been prophetic. He had said farewell.

The summer months were protracted agony for Robertson, despite the care and tenderness that encircled him. Throbbing pains in his head made life simply endurance. Light tortured his eyes. Sounds were all clash and jangle. Paralysis crept into the legs that once gathered mile after mile, and jumped nimbly across ditch and over hedge. Now he dragged himself through the house from bed to sofa, from sofa to chair, and along the wall from one piece of furniture to the next. Sometimes he ventured outside, where he toddled a few yards back and forth in the sun. But other days he could hardly trek across the bedroom.

Movements in the household gave way to the needs of the invalid. Mrs. Robertson, the doctors, and friends did what they could to ease his suffering. On the doctor's side were such medicines as morphine, quinine, citrate of iron, while family and friends came with luxuries such as ice and "recherché soups sent from all quarters." Robertson deadened the pain with patience. There was also another Comforter. "It is not in the day of high health and strength, when our intellect is powerful, our memory vigorous, when we feel strong in our integrity and courage, but when our weakened powers have made us feel that we are 'a worm and no man'; when our failing faculties convince us that, except for our connection with immortality, our minds would be as nothing; when we feel temptation getting too strong for us, and that we are on the brink of falling—then it is that we are taught there is a strength not our own, beyond anything that we possess of our own. It is then that the presence of the Son of Man is felt; then is the day of our merciful deliverance."

At times Robertson's strength seemed to flicker into a higher flame, but only as the guttering of a dying candle. After four weeks of respite from preaching, he wrote a letter that showed his mind quickening to an old scientific interest. "I send you a letter of Faraday's, published in *The Times*, which gave me pleasure, because it assigns, almost in my words, precisely the same origin to table-turning, etc., which I had discovered; because, too, the principle of the test invented by Faraday is exactly the same as that which I applied to Rutter's imaginary discovery, and because his remarks at the end coincide with the opinion which I have so often expressed about the false and ignorant state of the public mind which these endless credulities and restlessnesses betoken."

But his fingers scarcely had the strength to grip the pen. He sent another letter on the same day. This time he wrote from a reclining position, and used a pencil, which he said would not splutter and blot. In this note he gave "a facetious sketch of my highly useful life": "Hot milk as soon as I awake, to prevent fainting. An hour's siesta. Up. Interesting contest between F. W. R. and a fainting fit. Faint says, 'I have you.' 'Not yet,' says F. W. R., looking like a ghastly turnip, and falls into a cold bath, a splash whereof robs Faint of his prey. Manful attempts at drying. Operation just concluded; back comes the white demon. F. W. R. falls on the bed, reflecting strangely on supported vertebral column, and congratulating himself on his profound knowledge of anatomy. Ten minute elapse. F. W. R. fortifies himself with two spoonfuls of citrate of ammonia, on the strength of which he goes on triumphantly till the barbarous operation of shaving comes, in the middle of which Faint shouts, with a provoking little squeak, 'He! He! He!' So much for anatomy, and down goes F. W. R."

The first real improvement—also the last—came in August. "I take advantage of the first rally to write a few lines to you to give an account of myself. Yesterday, after a few hours' sleep I had a sudden and surprising rally; and though I am as weak as water, and can scarcely move a few yards without sighing and sobbing like a baby, I do trust in God I have turned the corner. Such an illness I never had before, and hope never to have again. For twenty-four hours I thought all was over, and Dr. Allen frankly told me he had ceased to be sanguine of my recovery.

2 P.M.

"I was obliged to give up writing from exhaustion. I try again. How far the brain is injured God only knows. It is the great *ganglia* or bunches of nerves which are at the roots of the brain that are affected. For many days I have not stirred from my bed, and a hideous-looking ourang-outang I am. [Doctors] Taylor, Whitehouse, Allen—the latter twice, Taylor once—every day; and, as if that were not enough, they have sent for Watson from town. He will be here this evening. God has treated me very mercifully. That I have felt in the direst pain and deepest exhaustion—the house filled with delicacies, presents which I cannot use, however. How different from the lot of Him who would fain 'have slaked His morning hunger on green figs!' I have not been allowed to see any one. Lady Byron left a sick-bed ten days ago to come to see me, and I have only once conversed with her for three minutes. Again I am dizzy, and must stop. I am broken as I never was before; but by God's mercy I may recover now—nay, even rapidly."

Then on August 12 he scratched a note that seemed torn from his mind, rough-edged, incomplete, but with swift eloquence announcing the end of life. "I have grown worse and worse every day for the last fortnight. From intensity of suffering in the brain, and utter powerlessness and prostration too dreadful to describe, and the acknowledged anxiety of the medical men, I think now that I shall not get over this. His will be done! I write in torture."

That word, "torture," with his name scrawled under it, was the last he ever wrote. Robertson neither cared nor was able to record the stages of the anguish. He lingered for three days. There were no heroics and no oratory. One who for thirteen years had knelt by so many deathbeds—"timid women and resolute men, quietly watching their own decay and fronting death unflinchingly"—did not fear to meet his God.

Sunday, August 15, 1853, marked the sixth anniversary

of Robertson's coming to Brighton. He lived through the day. When his friends at Trinity Chapel heard that he was sinking fast, there were prayers for him, wrung from hearts that he had turned to God. They shed tears for six years of remembrance. In the house on Montpelier Road, the pastor's life ebbed away. He was moved to an open window, where he rested until the cool of evening. About ten o'clock the pangs hit with double force. The eleventh hour went by, with pain in every pulse. In the final agony he uttered the prayer, "My God, my Father—My God, my Father!"

His wife, his mother, and a friend, along with the doctors, watched over him at the end. There were two hours of torture. His brain hurt, it hurt, only God knew how it hurt. The friends tried to relieve his suffering by moving him. He winced at the slightest touch. He said, "I cannot bear it; let me rest. I must die. Let God do His work." That was all. Midnight came. A few minutes later he died.

The family wished to have a private ceremony, but the members of Trinity Chapel and the citizens of Brighton claimed that Frederick Robertson had also belonged to them. The working men, the Athenaeum, and other societies of the town formally expressed their sorrow to the Robertsons, and asked for the privilege of marching in the funeral procession. The family could not refuse this "homage paid to goodness."

On Monday, August 23, the cortege began to move slowly toward the new Extramural Cemetery, a quiet place northward of Brighton. More than fifteen hundred men walked with the body, forming a procession nearly half a mile in length. Along the route from Montpelier Road to the cemetery shops were closed, windows curtained, and many of the people who crowded the pavements and verandahs were dressed in mourning. Rich and poor, conservatives and liberals were there, not only from Trinity Chapel, but other High and Low Church Anglicans, Nonconformists, Roman Catholics, Jews, Quakers, and Unitarians, all mingled indistinguishably together. English reserve did not display its sorrow, but the faces of the people showed the solemnity of the hour. The funeral gave them pause to think of the man who had stood by his ideals in the midst of criticism and abuse. Robertson was gone, and for a day at least Brighton was no longer Brighton. So the body passed to the place of rest, with the highest honor that the living can pay the dead, the tribute of silence and grief.

The Anglican clergymen of Brighton, along with ministers of other Protestant groups, waited for the procession at the gateway of the cemetery. The multitude went to the grave, where the last prayers were said, with the triumphant passage, "O death, where is thy sting? O grave, where is thy victory? The sting of death is sin; and the strength of sin is the law. But thanks be to God, which giveth us the victory through our Lord Jesus Christ." They laid him to rest in the hollow of the hill. Above him were the fresh slopes of the downs. Below lay Brighton. The sea-scented winds blew over his grave, and beyond moved the sea, where the voice of many waters sang his requiem.

XV

The Lasting Appeal of the Preacher

FREDERICK WILLIAM ROBERTSON began life with no special privilege of title or advantage of wealth. He did not win academic distinction, and he did not hold an honorary degree. As a minister in the Church of England, he received no preferment, gained no wealthy patronage, formed no party, held no office, and wrote no scholarly or popular books. His influence did not reach far beyond Brighton. He never delivered a sermon at the University in Oxford, his *alma mater*, or in Cambridge. He never filled the pulpit at St. Paul's or Westminster. He never was honored with a chaplaincy. He never preached at Court. Robertson died young—and by certain measurements he fell far short of success.

It is sad to think how large a task remained for him to do, and what funds of unspent thought still were in him when he died. The shortness of his ministry has made his lasting appeal a wonder. The nineteenth century heard many excellent spokesmen of religion, Anglican, Nonconformist, and Roman Catholic, but which of these would have become famous had he died at thirty-seven? Would Thomas Chalmers, who at that age had scarcely begun to write the sermons that

are the glory of the Scottish pulpit? Or John Henry Newman, who had published only half his tracts? What of Maurice and Mozley? What of Irving, Farrar, Wilberforce,
Magee, and Liddon? Had they died so young, would Phillips
Brooks, Horace Bushnell, or Henry Ward Beecher be well
remembered by ministers today? We may set down Spurgeon
as an exception, for he spoke with as much force at twenty-
three as at fifty-three. But all of these men lived and worked
through mature years. Any one of them enjoyed a wider
reputation during his lifetime, but probably none did so
much to change the history of preaching as Robertson of
Brighton.

He had finished his work at Trinity Chapel. A second
harvest followed the printing of his sermons. The Robertson
family put out the first four series between 1855 and 1859.
A reviewer in a Scottish journal remarked that a library
copy of the sermons was likely to be "thumbed, dog's-eared,
pencil-marked, worn with much perusal." A writer in the *Saturday Review* stated that "there are many persons, and the
number increases every year, to whom Robertson's writings
are the most stable, satisfactory, and exhaustless form of
religious teaching which the nineteenth century has given—
the most wise, suggestive, and practical." In America the
Atlantic Monthly predicted of Robertson: "It is hazarding
little to say that his volumes will take the rank of classics."

Moreover, the *Brighton Gazette*, which once had lampooned the preacher of Trinity Chapel, now honored the
prophet in his own country. "As an author, Mr. Robertson
was, in his lifetime, unknown; for with the exception of one
or two addresses, he never published, having a singular dis-
inclination to bring his thoughts before the public in the
form of published sermons. As a minister, he was beloved and

esteemed for his unswerving fidelity to his principles and his fearless propagation of his religious views. As a townsman, he was held in the highest estimation; his hand and voice being ever ready to do all in his power to advance the moral and social position of the working men. It was not till after his decease, which event created a sensation and demonstration such as Brighton never before or since witnessed, that his works were subjected to public criticism. It was then found that in the comparatively retired minister of Trinity Chapel there had existed a man possessed of consummate ability and intellect of the highest order; that the sermons laid before his congregation were replete with the subtleties of intellect, and bore evidence of the keenest perception and most exalted catholicity."

A young man, twenty-four years of age, had begun meanwhile to collect materials for the life of Robertson. For some time there had been hesitation in the choice of a biographer. The Robertson letters belonged mostly to people allied with the Broad Church movement; they wished to avoid casting a shadow on Robertson's position in the Church. These men had formed a high opinion of Stopford A. Brooke, a young Irishman fresh from college in Dublin, who bore the stamp of no religious party. He became their choice. Formerly Brooke had met Robertson in Brighton; now he came to know the preacher still more intimately. Brooke viewed his subject from every angle. He read the sermons, sorted and selected letters to and from Robertson, and made the best of every chance to talk with the family and friends of the preacher. He devoted eight years to the *Life and Letters of Fred. W. Robertson.*

When the book came out in 1865, Robertson's name, personality, and teaching began to shine in a new light. Brooke revealed that soul in all its amazing proportions. The Brighton preacher had been at once the loneliest and the most sympathetic of men. His character mingled unflinching courage with an "almost incredible shyness." He was both proud and modest; impulsive and longsuffering; a zealous reformer and a thinker of robust common sense. Robertson said, "My tastes are with the aristocrats, my principles with the mob." Action suited his nature, but he lived a contemplative life. He did not want to become a popular preacher, and yet he lavished hours of thought on every sermon. He was denied things that he most wished for, and granted things that he least desired. The union of so many apparent contradictions had drawn and repelled hearers, excited churchmen and disappointed them, won supporters and driven them away. The biography, however, clearly outlined a man large enough to assimilate these different forces, and then give them unity of purpose.

Reviewers at once acknowledged Brooke's work as a biography of rare skill and power. Four editions sold out in the first year. The reading public seldom had opportunity to learn of a man with such a passionate, sensitive heart as Robertson. The "inward martyr life" of this modern saint gave courage to many who had never known the young preacher of Brighton. Of course the *Record* still grumbled on one side; and on the other, Dean R. W. Church, author of a treatise on the Tractarians, delivered a tirade in his *Occasional Papers*. But in general, after the publication of the life, most criticism of Robertson lost its cutting edge.

Brooke rendered an even more valuable service in giving a key to the pulpit work of Robertson. The biography multiplied the sale of the *Sermons*, and the *Sermons* quickened interest in the biography. Arthur Penrhyn Stanley, whose *Life and Correspondence of Thomas Arnold* has become a biographical landmark, counseled Brooke in writing the story of Robertson's life. He thought the narrative exceedingly well done, yet he said: "Deep as is the interest of reading it, the sermons still seem the climax of the man."

Toward the end of the century, Stanley himself wrote an article in which he said of Robertson: "He was a contemporary of mine at Oxford; but I have not the slightest recollection of ever having heard his name at that time. He was also curate at St. Ebbe's in Oxford during some part of my stay there; but neither did I then become acquainted with him, nor, in fact, ever hear that such a person existed. In later years I now and then heard of his fame at Brighton; but I never was there on Sunday, and therefore my early ignorance of him was never compensated by any knowledge in later times. How remarkable is the contrast of this obscurity with his wide-spread popularity in after years! It is not too much to say that he has become, beyond question, the greatest preacher of the nineteenth century, and with the most powerful reasons for this wide-spread judgment."

Robertson's *Sermons*, nearly a hundred years after he preached them, are still in print. They continue to move many readers, because the Brighton preacher offers a message to our times. According to the late Barrett Wendell, of Harvard, literature is writing that lives on after the conditions that produced it have passed away. If so, Robertson stands out as a master. At present he is the one preacher whom the lover of this art can study with most profit. Robertson's world has gone. Events that prompted him to speak have passed away, his co-laborers have died, and most of the issues with which he and they wrestled have changed form or else have been forgotten. Robertson preached to his own congregation and for his own day. Yet many of his sermons seem as winning now as when the first volume broke into print.

Most of all, these sermons still appeal to thinking Christians because of their "biblicalness." Robertson made a habit of going straight to the Bible as the main source of materials. Whether he preached a textual sermon, or an expository, he looked on himself as an interpreter. He lived for aims like those of men in the Bible; he suffered as they had suffered. He brought to the Scriptures talents of scholarship, imagination, "logic on fire," and a sensitive awareness that in these pages God was speaking to his condition. As an interpreter he combined gifts not often found in a single person: his work, as a whole, excels in thought, feeling, and power. As much as any other minister of modern times, Robertson demonstrates the fruitfulness of preaching from the Bible.

Doctrine interested Robertson. Like the philosopher Lessing, he thought that he saw the difference between the "orthodoxist" and orthodoxy. With deep conviction he urged unity among Christians. None the less, he apparently held Evangelicalism to be little more than a scheme for snatching men from judgment. He overlooked the deeper Evangelical view of Christ's work—Christ the Deliverer, not only from punishment, but also from sin itself; removing the power of guilt, not only by His suffering, but also by giving the believer endurance to work out his own salvation. The present writer, along with many other ministers today, admires Robertson without going all lengths with him in everything that he says. He had blind spots. His sermons live, however, because of what he believed, constructively, and the fervency with which he made known his faith.

In theology Robertson appeals to us by his fresh interpretation of Christian thought. He assented only to the duty of preaching Christ. Therefore he did not hesitate to brush away cobwebs of custom. He wished to preach as Christ preached: "God—man—immortality." He said that doctrine is important, and liturgy has its place, but unless these are felt as well as accepted, they have no value. Religious affections mean vastly more than shibboleths of party religion. "Who is the true man?" asked Robertson. "He who does the truth; and never holds a principle on which he is not prepared in any hour to act, and in any hour to risk the consequences of holding it."

Courage marked the words of Robertson, especially in his ethical teaching, when he dealt with the social crisis of his age. He held out to his congregation the summons of unexpected thought. The growing numbers of "cheated people" forced him to speak of the chasm that lay between the privileged and the poor. His boldness emerged from other topics as well. The heritage of spiritual bewilderment, greed of novelty and lust of change, intellectual pride and grasping materialism, cruel self-interest and heartless penance, flimsy virtue and deep-rooted vice—these faced Robertson no less than the man of God today.

What held Robertson in Brighton? Duty kept him there. The Apostle Paul wrote the Corinthians that he hoped to visit them; but not yet. He felt bound to stay at Ephesus: "A great door and effectual is opened unto me, and there are many adversaries." Robertson commented: "Ephesus was his post, and at Ephesus he would stay. Moreover, the very circumstance which to many would have been an inducement to depart, was with St. Paul a strong one to remain: there were 'many adversaries,' and he was there to take part in danger." The same combativeness showed up in Robertson. Until he saw some of the chasms bridged between class and class, and wounds in process of healing, his work in Brighton was not yet done. Trinity Chapel was his post; he would not desert; rather he would preach all the more fervently. His faith did not falter in the midst of uncertain ways.

The message of Robertson deserves to live also because it reveals a hard-won victory over anguish of body and of soul. Pain was almost sacred to him, for Christ was made "perfect through sufferings." How could one who went through such torment prepare such sermons? An ordinary man would have capitulated. Robertson struggled on. He was still at heart a soldier. Duty braced him. Sometimes he thought of Elijah under his juniper tree, and wished his wish to die. But he held fast to the need for a living sacrifice. He said that the hour comes when the true minister recognizes that law as God's will for himself. Then he voluntarily obeys. He can bless others when he gives up thoughts of his own comfort; he can help others when he thinks no longer of himself. Few sermons have cost so much in physical agony—spiritual travail—as those of Robertson. If for no other reason, his words call for study now because of their background in suffering.

The lasting appeal of Robertson depends in no small measure on his understanding of the human heart. He knew his own inner being. Furthermore, he had read widely and he had lived among men. These elements entered into the biographical sermons. He owed much to books: the philosophers helped him to range thoughts under general principles; the historians shed light on the past; the poets taught him the mysteries of the heart. But Robertson had a more direct knowledge of what is in man. He declared that no class of humans (except possibly the Epicureans, and he would exclude not even them) lay beyond the circle of his fellow-feeling. He teaches us above all to sympathize with everyone who suffers. The evidence of an understanding heart is at once the highest and deepest, the most certain and most elusive quality of his preaching. It cannot be explained; it can only be felt.

Many pastors today are concerned about spiritual ailments. In Robertson they should discover a sane, helpful guide. He has led the way as the first and best of "psychological preachers." Long before the method became current, he used individual "cases" to fasten his thought in the hearer's memory. Unlike some ministers of recent times, he took a large number of cases from the Scriptures. In "The Parable of the Sower" he cited Judas, Martha, Lot, Hannah, and Elijah as examples of his teaching. Elsewhere he drew from daily life. Listen to him in "The Principle of the Spiritual Harvest":

"The conscientious churchman complains that his delicate scruples or his bold truthfulness stand in the way of his preferment while another man, who conquers his scruples and softens the eye of truth, rises, and sits down a mitred peer in Parliament. The honorable lawyer feels that his practice is limited, while the unprincipled practitioner receives all he loses; and the Christian physician feels sore and sad at perceiving that charlatanism succeeds in winning employment; or, if not charlatanism, at least that affability and courtly manners take the place that is due to superior knowledge. . . .

"But you have resolved to be a liver—a doer—a champion of the truth. Your ambition is to be pure in the last recesses of the mind. You have your reward: a soul upright and manly—a fearless bearing, that dreads to look no man in the face—a willingness to let men search you through and through, and defy them to see any difference between what you seem and what you are. Now, your price: your price is dislike. The price of being true is the Cross. The warrior of the truth must not expect success. What have you to do with

190 *The Soul of Frederick W. Robertson*

popularity? Sow for it, and you will have it. But if you wish for it, or wish for peace, you have mistaken your calling; you must not be a teacher of the truth; you must not cut prejudice against the grain: you must leave medical, legal, theological truth, to harder and nobler men, who are willing to take the martyr's cross, and win the martyr's crown. This is the mistake men make. They expect both harvests, paying only one price."

Through the sermons of Robertson we have the privilege of his company. We may claim the right to share his deepest thought and experience, and to partake of his suffering. In view of his life, one may have a sense of incompleteness. But this sense tends to fade when one lives with the sermons; for in them Robertson left the signs not only of promise but of fulfillment. Although he died young, there lingers now the impression of a finished life. Robertson of Brighton offers us the companionship of his greatness—great not merely for what he said, but also for what he was, and for what he had the power of helping others to become. Being dead, he yet speaks to us in the last words of "The Loneliness of Christ":

"The practical result and inference of all this is a very simple, but a very deep one—the deepest of existence. Let life be a life of faith. Do not go timorously about, inquiring what others think, what others believe, and what others say. It seems the easiest, it is the most difficult thing in life, to do this—believe in God. God is near you. Throw yourself fearlessly upon Him. Trembling mortal, there is an unknown might within your soul, which will wake when you command it. The day may come when all that is human, man and woman, will fall off from you, as they did from Christ. Let His strength be yours. Be independent of them all now. The Father is with you. Look to Him, and He will save you."

A Selected Robertson Bibliography

Arnold, Frederick. *Robertson of Brighton.* London: Ward and Downey, 1886. (A discursive, often pointless, biography.)

Blackwood, Andrew W. *Preaching in Time of Reconstruction.* Great Neck, N. Y.: The Pulpit Press, 1945. (A chapter on "The Sermons of a Soldier—Frederick W. Robertson.")

Brastow, Lewis O. *Representative Modern Preachers.* Cincinnati: Jennings and Graham, 1910. (Chapter 2: "Frederick William Robertson.")

Brooke, Stopford A. *Life and Letters of Fred. W. Robertson.* London: Smith, Elder, and Co., 1865. (The definitive biography.)

Buchan, John. "Nine Brasenose Worthies" in *Brasenose College Quatercentenary Monographs,* XIX Century. Oxford: The Clarendon Press, Vol. II, Part 2, 1909. (Robertson is among the "worthies.")

Cambridge History of English Literature, The Nineteenth Century, ed. by A. W. Ward. New York: G. P. Putnam's Sons, 1916. (Chapter 13—"The Growth of Liberal Theology"—gives an excellent appraisal of Robertson's work and influence.)

Church, R. W. *Occasional Papers.* London: The Macmillan Co., 1897. (Church was High Anglican; he did not admire Robertson. In this book he strongly criticized the minister of Brighton.)

Currier, Albert H. *Nine Great Preachers.* Boston: The Pilgrim Press, 1912. (The author calls Robertson "the most remarkable English preacher of the nineteenth century.")

Davis, Ozora S. *Principles of Preaching.* Chicago: University of Chicago Press, 1929. (Reprint of "Obedience the Organ of Spiritual Knowledge," with study questions.)

Edwards, John. *Nineteenth Century Preachers.* London: Charles H. Kelly, 1902. (The second chapter is on "F. W. Robertson.")

Henson, H. Hensley. *Church and Parson in England.* London: Hodder and Stoughton, 1927. (Chapter 3: "Robertson of Brighton.")

———. *Robertson of Brighton.* London: Smith, Elder, and Co., 1916. (Published on the centenary of Robertson's birth.)

Hoppin, James M. *Homiletics.* New York: Funk and Wagnalls, 1883. (The good and bad points of Robertson's preaching, with stress on the good.)

Howard, Harry C. *Princes of the Christian Pulpit and Pastorate.* Nashville: Abingdon-Cokesbury Press, 1927. (Chapter 8 deals with the life and preaching of Robertson.)

Jacks, L. P. *Life and Letters of Stopford Brooke.* London: John Murray, 1917. (The author warns against the interpretation of Robertson by Stopford Brooke, especially in Chapter 7 of *Life and Letters of Fred. W. Robertson.*)

Lewis, Benjamin (Lewis Melville, pseud.) *Brighton.* London: Chapman and Hall, 1909. (A careful study describing the history, follies, and fashions of Brighton.)

Library of Literary Criticism, ed. by Charles W. Moulton. Buffalo: The Moulton Publishing Company, Vol. V, 1902. (Brief critical estimates by various men concerning Robertson's life and ministry.)

McComb, Samuel. *Preaching in Theory and Practice.* New York: Oxford University Press, 1926. (Dedicated to Frederick W. Robertson and Stopford A. Brooke.)

Mark, Thiselton. *The Pedagogics of Preaching.* New York: Fleming H. Revell Co., 1911. (Analysis of the sermon on "The Early Development of Jesus.")

Morley, Edith J. *The Life and Times of Henry Crabb Robinson.* London: J. M. Dent and Sons Ltd., 1935.

Pressensé, Edmond de. *Contemporary Portraits.* New York: A. D. F. Randolph and Co., 1880. (Robertson as a theologian.)

Robertson, Frederick W. *Analysis of Mr. Tennyson's "In Memoriam."* London: Kegan Paul, Trench and Co., 1882.

————. *Expository Lectures on St. Paul's Epistles to the Corinthians.* London: Smith, Elder and Co., 1859.

————. *The Human Race, And Other Sermons.* London: Kegan Paul, Trench and Co., 1883.

————. *Lectures and Addresses,* On Literary and Social Topics. London: Smith, Elder and Co., 1858.

————. *Notes on Genesis.* London: Henry S. King and Co., 1877.

————. *Sermons,* Preached at Trinity Chapel, Brighton. London: Smith, Elder and Co. (The *Sermons* came out in five series: the first and second in 1855; others in 1857, 1859, and 1890. These works have passed through countless editions. Harper & Brothers now sell the five series in a single volume.)

Robinson, Henry Crabb. *Diary, Reminiscences, and Correspondence.* London: The Macmillan Co., 1869. (Many references to Robertson, found neither in Brooke's nor in Arnold's biography.)

Smyth, Charles. *The Art of Preaching*. London: Society for the Promotion of Christian Knowledge, 1940. (The author puts Robertson in the very front rank of English preachers. The book contains an analysis of "The Skepticism of Pilate.")

Sutton, Filbert. *Faith and Science*. London: Bell and Daldy, 1868. (A chapter on the writing and character of Robertson.)

Young, Julian Charles. *Last Leaves from the Journal of Julian Charles Young*. Edinburgh: Edmonston and Douglas, 1875. (A personal recollection of Robertson; the writer was a fellow clergyman.)

Index

195